COINSHOOTING II

DIGGING DEEPER COINS

H. Glenn Carson

The chapters in this book are articles written for the different Treasure Hunting Magazines. I apologize for statements that seem repetitious, but some things in this hobby field need repeating.
H. Glenn Carson

FREE Treasure Reference Catalog.   **Dealer Discounts available.**

printed by
CARSON ENTERPRISES
Drawer 71, Deming, NM 88031-0071
ⓒ **1982 by Carson Enterprises, Ltd.**
ISBN 0-941620-17-4

CONTENTS

Cover photo was taken by Mr. Bob Tinsley, publisher of *TOWNS WEST MAGAZINE*, published in Odessa, Texas.

Artifacts courtesy of Harley Smith, Jim Blain of Fireball Electronics, Inc. and R.W. Umstot.

The cap and ball pistol "Black Powder" was recovered by an old man near Abilene, Texas while using his metal detector and brought to Harley Smith. Jim Pilaska found one of the gold coins near Popes Crossing on the Pecos River in Texas, and Harley Smith found the civil war military buttons at Horsehead Crossing and Pontoon Crossing on the Pecos River. The letter "A" defined the "A" Company of the military around 1865-66. The rifle used later by the military in this area.

---photo courtesy of Harley Smith,
          Fireball Electronics, Odssa, Texas.

METAL DETECTORS -

Coinshooting would not be much of a hobby without the magic electronic wand. It is the primary tool of the trade. Even so, let nobody kid you. It is the person using the detector that determines the results gained in this hobby field. The least expensive detector, in the hands of a person who knows how to use it, and does so, can produce some amazing results. The best detector can seem to be a dud if not well-used.

No attempt will be made here to give all the details of all the detectors. There are some very good detectors these days. Some excellent changes have come about in just the past few years. Starting with VLF circuitry, deeper coins began to come up. It was tough using those early units, for ferrous materials were read at tremendous depths. Many a coin-shooter gave up on those units, tired of digging up rusted bits of nails at fourteen inches or more. Then discrimination on the deeper seekers began to creep in, and those who learned to use those first units began to make some remarkable finds.

If you get your local dealers to demonstrate the latest models, you will find that it is no longer necessary to whip that unit around like a scythe at hay-cutting time to get good readings. That was the problem with those earlier deep-reading discriminators. You wore your arm out whipping that loop back and forth, or developed muscles like Popeye.

Today's detectors, if one takes the time to learn how to use them efficiently, can be an endless source of satisfaction. Don't kid yourself, though. They still take work, determination, thought, and persistence. You need to learn what that detector will and will not do, and that comes with practice and seeking out answers that only actual hunting can give.

If you are thinking of getting a new detector, shop around. Try several, read the current ads, talk to several dealers if at all possible. Preferably, deal with a more local person, so you can actually see how various units work. If a person says, "THIS is the best one, the only one," take it with a grain of salt. Make him prove it to you.

By all means, get the best detector you can afford. Learn how to use it. It will be the key to endless hours of pleasurable hunting.

SMALL TALK ON DEEP DIGGING

Small talk is well worth listening to when it comes to coinshooting, for often it is the feeble sounds, the little indications which indicate the better coins you'll find. The big brazen noises your detector makes most often speak of various junk, at or near the surface. True, that includes the clad tokens that pass as coinage these days. There's a good many small, random things to know about coinshooting, though, that remain unrecognized or unrealized at the fringes of the obvious. These paragraphs attempt to deal with such small talk, bringing together some rather unrelated ideas that nevertheless are important to each other. It's done with the hope it is not just trivia: if it helps, it won't be just small talk, afterall.

We'll whisper this, for it is the feeblest sounds to which a coinshooter must train himself to hear. The weak, the almost unperceived, the tiniest sounds are best. This is true no matter what sort of detector a person is using, for such signals indicate objects down at the lowest penetration capabilities of that detector. Discriminators, standard units, or the new mineralization-ignorers, they all say the sweetest things when they murmur the lowest. If you train your hearing and mind to pay the most attention to those lesser sounds, your recovery of older, deeper objects will improve.

Nothing is too simple, and that does include coin-shooting! Many people gain that mistaken impression just after they begin to learn their detector. Your search is affected by the varying conditions of the soils in which you must work. The same place does not always have the same kind of soil conditions, either, for moisture, evaporation of moisture, heat, and cold can all change how your detector, and you, react. Mineralization affects detection far, far more than most people realize. Nearby electrical lines and motors can adversely affect detection. Among the most overlooked facts of all is how the burrowing activities of various small animals, constantly going on, can affect coinshooting.

The earthworm is a lowly creature, and most TH-ers probably never give the little critters much, if any thought, nor any of the other things that wriggle around below the surface. This neglect does not alter the fact that earthworms and other such things do indeed have much to do with deeper coins, or at least how they got to be deeper. Pressure, vibration, and soil buildup can only bury a coin or any other metalic artifact so deep. Things do not sink on their own in most soils. Something else has to move objects deeper. Pressure can drive a coin deeply into the soil, especially if the soil is loose, muddy, or other-wise soft. Someone or something, such as sheepsfoot rollers used on many lawns, can and do force coins into the ground. Vibration <u>can</u> cause a coin to move downwards through the soil. Nearby traffic, con-struction, and engine vibrations are culprits. Soil <u>can</u> be added. It can be washed in, blown in, or deliberately added. All deep coins are not deep just because of these things, however, for other actions tend to move coins upwards. Soil blows away, it washes away, it is sometimes deliberately carried away. Frost heaves heavy objects surfacewards.

What about the earthworm and his friends, and how do they fit into the picture? The earthworm, a simple creature, feeds from decaying vegetation in the soil. A small, living auger, the worm literally eats its way through the soil. It digests the vegetable material in the soil and transports its waste material to the surface. Small but steady soil buildup, far exceeding soil blown or washed in in most places. Healthy soil has thousands of these small, busy tunnelers. They leave countless, criss-crossed cavities in the top foot or so of soil. Many such tunnels are bored each year underneath coins. Coins, being heavy, sink into these empty places, minute fractions of an inch at a time. Activity on the surface aids this collapse. Deeper and deeper go the coins.

The process is not rapid, its speed depends actually on how many worms there are in that particular soil. It is not deliberate, for the worms are only after whatever vegetable material is in the soil. As a coin sinks, the process slows. Less vegetable material is available the deeper a coin gets, and earthworms   have less and less reason to tunnel beneath it.

Larger burrowing creatures can drop coins far deeper into the ground. The tighter the soil and the less animal activity there is, the more shallow the coins will be. That is why many ghost town sites in hardpacked, dry areas have many shallow coins. Where mole, gopher, and other such digging creatures have been active over long years there really is no telling how deeply coins may be buried. Far beyond the detection range of most units to be sure!

The composition of the soil has a great deal to do with how deeply coins may be buried. Tight, heavy soils do not allow coins to sink easily, looser soils do. In looser soils the digging activities of small creatures is more intense. An old dime in dry, heavy clay may be three or four inches down, whereas in moist, loamy soil it may be well over a foot down.

One question seems to puzzle many coinshooters. The answer is uncomplicated, but still not obvious, until thought out. "Why can a person go back time after time to the same exact spot and still come up with deeper coins?" Do coins move around as the old Spanish thought? First, the coinshooter may not be gridding the area in different directions. Deep coins may give a signal from one direction, no signal at all from another direction. This is especially true if the coin is not horizontal, or at a slight angle to the surface. Second, and of even more importance, is what for lack of a better term could be called "the sawblade effect".

The detection pattern of any metal detector is cone-shaped. Right beneath the loop, the pattern is somewhat a wide circle, depending on what unit you have as to how wide. At the limit of the unit's range, several inches into the ground, the detection range has shrunk to a mere pin-point. How deep also depends upon which unit you have as well as the size of the detected object. To search deeper levels <u>completely</u> is a job nigh impossible. To do so, a coinshooter would have to overlap his sweeps far more tightly than most of any of us do. One or two inches is about all most people overlap their sweeps, and not that much when they get tired and careless. Some meticulous searchers overlap their sweeps three or four inches. A careful five or six inch overlap would be better, if you really want to fully scan to the fullest detection capabilities of your unit, and even that would not be complete.

What actually happens is that most of us leave huge dimensions of unscanned depths behind us. If one is searching, looking from the side and below ground level, the deeper, then the shallower detection penetrations would look much like a sawblade with wide, deepset teeth. There would be as much or more unsearched volume of soil in the peaks as that which had been searched in the valleys. Speed compounds the problem, for weak signals are easily missed. Knowing this fact should make one <u>slow down</u> if he is searching for the deeper, older coins.

It simply makes good sense.

Added to this problem is the fact that most "swaths", or widths of search areas are often not overlapped at all well. Large triangular areas are often left unsearched at the ends of swings, especially where coinshooters try to cover ground quickly. Worse, at the end of the swing, the detector loop often is allowed to come off the ground. Every inch into the air not only loses one inch, but more, because of the angle of the loop to the ground surface. Don't make your swings too wide!

Mineralization affects coinshooting far more than most people realized. Coins can be found far deeper by standard detectors in non-mineralized soils than in soil which has even slight metal content. Metallic salts, high iron content, and any number of elements in the soil can adversely affect an area for coinshooting. Only recently have several units been developed that detect objects deeply through such soils. Such units work on a very low frequency, and they are not inexpensive machines.

These units are not for the casual or careless coinshooter. They must be used with extreme care in areas of turf. They detect everything , and they go deep . These new machines detect tiny objects through mineralized soils at amazing depths. This sounds great, but the immense disadvantage to this soon becomes obvious. In many areas such units cannot be moved but a few inches without obtaining several signals. Some of the new discriminating units meet part of this challenge. Check several of them before you purchase one.

How then can a coinshooter not go crazy digging up everything that causes a signal, often at depths exceeding a foot? Such digging would soon close every public place to ALL coinshooting. The answer is two-fold, at least.

First, larger signals should be ignored, if you are truly interested in getting down to that which is older and deeper. It takes great self discipline to do this, ignoring signals, but it must be done. If you want MORE coins, and don't care if they are new, use a good discriminator. Ignoring signals while using a low frequency machine means missing many, many newer coins and some jewelry. It means going over some silver coins not too deeply buried. It also means you miss countless junk items near the surface when you concentrate on feeble signals indicating the older and deeper items.

Secondly, the art of probing must be mastered. With a foot-long probe, or one even longer, sounds must be pinpointed and the object carefully probed for. An electrician's screwdriver works reasonably well, or any long, sturdy steel tool that can be used as a probe. A brass-tipped probe is good in that it does not mar coins. It is bad in that the brass quickly wears away. Careful probing will not ruin too many coins. Careless probing can cost you tens and hundreds of dollars a thrust! Remember, too, such a tool is only a probe, not something with which to pry. What you seek is too deep to do that let alone the harm it will do the coin.

Thrust slowly and evenly, exactly above where you believe the signal to center. You will feel the article if it is there. It may take several probes, moving around from the original spot, but if something is there, you will feel it. With practice you can tell the difference between rocks, clumps of foil, most bottle caps, and coins. It does take practice. If it can't be felt do you really want to dig a hole a foot or more in depth?

Once you know that something is there, then a hole must be dug. Take care! Cut as small a surface plug as possible with as much root volume as possible. It should be large enough in diameter to allow your hand and forearm to enter. Put the plug and dirt onto a cloth or plastic piece so that it may be dumped back into the hole when you finish. Dig around the outside of the hole as you go down. A knife or a narrow-bladed trowel is good for this purpose. Any sturdy, flat-bladed tool. You may need to have a tool holder of some kind to carry on your belt or around a shoulder. Otherwise you end up carrying a lot of stuff besides your detector, and that is not good. The cloth can be carried in your pocket or in the nail apron every coinshooter should wear for collecting the trash dug up. This apron can be adapted as a tool carrier, too.

If this sounds like too much work, forget about deeper, older coins. The crew that takes shovels into city parks, schoolyards, and other such sodded areas is going to close down coinshooting in that area in a big hurry, for everybody. No consience, soon no coinshooting. It is not a lot of work at all when one considers the rewards of older, fascinating, and valuable finds such efforts enables one to RECOVER, and recover in the best possible shape if done correctly.

There is not an older community in the country where such techniques will not prove to be of value to one who takes the time to master them. The "worked-over" and "worked-out" areas are often the very best spots, too. The newer stuff has been removed. Much of the trash is already gone. There are fewer loud signals to ignore. In such clean areas you   might even want to probe for louder signals, too.

Earphones are a MUST for this type of hunting. Be sure to find a comfortable sound level so that the louder signals do not hurt your ears. Loud sounds not only are painful, they are hard on your ears and hearing. The earphones block out all sorts of external noise and allow you to concentrate on the tiny sounds. You can ignore traffic, wind, and, to some extent, even little kids.

This technique, or various adaptations of it suited to individuals and the soils in which they must work, have been and are working around the country right now. One man in Denver recently recovered an almost uncirculated 1899 Barber half dollar from Cheesman   Park. Another man found a seated liberty quarter, in fine condition, at 22 inches in Berkeley Park. Both men belong to the Eureka Club of Denver, a fine organization if you're ever through Denver on the second Friday evening of any month and want to meet some great detector fans. These parks were full of mineralized conditions ranging from bad to worse, by the way. Three large antique gold charms, twenty dollar gold piece size, were dug out of a park in Des Moines. Set in one charm was a large diamond. A jeweler offered the gal who found it $2500 on the spot when he saw it. She declined and later found he'd been willing to go about 40% of the gem's true value. An Estes Park coinshooter recently found an 1856 2½ dollar gold piece at an old New Mexico way station. One of the author's close "friends" this past fall dug a fine 1907 $5.00 gold piece out of Boulder's Chautauqua Park, another of those long "worked-over spots". On and on. These recoveries are strictly due to people learning more about deeper digging techniques.

It is not just Civil War Relics that are coming out of the ground with these new machines. One has to learn to use these new detectors, though, just as we had to learn how to use the detectors of a short few years ago. Persistence is even more important than it used to be, and so is coinshooting conscience. Try to find out what the various machines will do before you rush out and buy, then put a good deal of thoughtful practice into using the unit you finally purchase. It will pay off multifold.

If you also have a good discriminator, it will be well worthwhile to go over an area you wish to hunt with that first, and carefully. That way you will remove most of the top coins and can more blissfully ignore the loud sounds you encounter later. It will be rather hard on someone else not using these techniques who chooses to hunt that spot, but that won't be your problem.

These ideas hopefully hang together, and have been presented in the hope they will be of help to coinshooters. Perhaps they will. If we meet out there somewhere, and not too many coins are coming up at the time, how about us grabbing up a few of those little ol' worms and going fishing? We might catch us some supper, and besides, those particular little devils won't drop any more coins deeper into the ground than they already are.

DEFT DIGGING DISCUSSION

The worst threat to the coinshooting hobby these days is the poor to downright terrible digging techniques employed by far too many THers. It is a problem that could destroy the hobby for everybody. Careless and messy methods are causing more and more park officials, civic leaders, police personnel, and others responsible for the maintenance of various grounds to deal with increasing harshness towards coinshooters, the careful ones along with the unknowing and the indifferent. Most THers are careful, conscientious folks who want to do things right, and strive to do so, and this article is intended as a broadcasting of a few helpful hints as to how better to remove coins without harming lawn surface.

It is not enough to just say, "Fill in your holes". Most people do, but that is in itself not enough. Many holes are dug that do not need to be dug. Most parks soon show the effects of hole digging, especially in dry weather. Anyone who takes a shovel or a large trowel into a carefully tended lawn area should be, and probably will be told to leave. Such confrontations unfortunately also reflect on other hobbyists, many of whom are probably leaving little trace of their digging.

There is no one perfect digging method. Coins near the surface can usually be taken from the soil with little or no evidence of their departure. A screwdriver or a hunting knife will pop them right up, and few soil particles need remain visible. Back the tool a half inch or so away from the coin, after gently probing for it and centering it. Never jab fast and furiously. You don't need to. A soft touch will allow you to better feel the coin, and a savage thrust will mar the good and better coins.

Careful probing with a brass-tipped screwdriver
can locate objects below the surface. The proper
digging tools can leave very little evidence that
anything was ever recovered in a certain spot.

Pry up and back. The coin will show in the upturn-
ed earth. Remove it and tamp any loose soil back
into the silt. Step on the spot firmly. This method
does little to hurt grassy areas, and hardly shows
the spot was disturbed.

Always check the spot for additional coins before
moving on. Many times there is more than one coin
in one location. Often two or more coins are found
together.

The deeper the coins, the tougher the problem.
The deeper coins are the ones that most people desire. Such coins tend to be older. Those deep
ones are what causes deeper holes to be dug. Don't
give up, and don't just splash-dash in shovel and
pick, for it can be done well and unobtrusively.

There is no one way in either detecting or in digging coins. Soil conditions vary in all sorts of ways.
Varying moisture content, mineralization, plant cover,
rock, clay, humus, sand, and content, and tempera-
ture all can alleviate or compound the difficulty of
digging, let alone detecting. Work on the typical
problems in your own area, first, of course, but be
prepared for meeting up with all sorts of conditions
elsewhere.

Sandy or loamy soil is easiest to dig in, if it is
not too dry or too loose, or covered with some tough
grass such as Bermuda. The sides cave in badly if
it is too dry. In any deeper digging it is a good idea
to have along, perhaps carried in your nail/trash
apron, a square of cloth or plastic. Any loose dirt
can be put on this material, and returned into the '
hole when finished. It makes being neat simple.

Probing is a must in deep digging. If you cannot
find the coin, especially when using a conventional
detector, there probably is little use in digging the
hole. You also can safely ignore the very loud
sounds if interested primarily in the deeper coins.
You will miss newer coins near the top, but increase
your take of older material, if you listen and react only
on the more feeble sounds.

One of the best possible probes is an annealed
brass rod. A welding rod will do nicely. Affix some

kind of handle. A golf ball or tennis ball taped securely on the end of the rod will work well. Don't sharpen the rod. The soil will soon enough round it after continued probing. The brass will not mar coins in the severe manner ice picks or screwdrivers do, although those, too, will serve as good probes if a person has a soft enough touch. Remember, too, the probe is not for prying. A bent rod or two should teach one that quickly enough.

In digging shallower holes, probing and then slitting the grass is the better method, as a rule. If careful probing determines a deeper coin or other item, cutting a small plug may become necessary.

The best way to cut a plug is not to do it, if at all possible, especially in dry weather. If you must, to extract something deep, try to do it as neatly as possible, with minimum damage to the lawn. Cut as small a plug as possible, perhaps three inches in diameter, and only on three sides. Lay the plug, dirt-side up, trapdoor fashion, back away from the hole. The dirt beneath it then can be removed after checking both the plug and the hole with the detector to see if there is still something on deeper. Use that piece of cloth or plastic. Take the dirt out carefully, so as not to mar the coin, digging down around the outside edges of the hole. The hole can be enlarged as one goes deeper without widening the surface hole.

Check the removed dirt, for often the coin will come out in the middle of a clump if you are working only around the edges. This is what you want, for you won't be gouging and scratching the coin.

When the object is removed, return the loose soil you have on the cloth, and tamp it into the hole. The cloth makes this easy to do, and few stray particles of soil are left to point out your digging. Brush any dirt that does escape back into the hole and lay back the plug, hopefully still attached by that fourth side. This allows quicker regrowth of the grass. Step on the plug firmly, making certain it is level with the surrounding surface.

All this sounds much more time-consuming than it is. The hole must be dug if you want what is at the bottom of it. It does not take as long to fill in the hole as it did to dig it. Park personnel will not hate to see you, nor will they come over mad enough to toss you out on your ear.

In some areas that get very dry during certain seasons, such as some summers in the midwest, many long-time coinshooters even go to the length of carrying large water jugs in their vehicles. They can then put a cupful or more on their plug. It joins the dirt back together and when wetter weather returns the plugged area is as healthy, if not more so, than the surrounding grass.

There are places to use shovels and other large digging tools, but well-maintained lawn areas are not those places. The beaches, the open field, the pasture, and all sorts of boondocky places allow spadesful of earth to be turned over, especially if they are returned into place. In parks it is insanity, even if one sneaks in and gets away with it. Heavy digging tools are nearly as bad as shovels in parks. Even the hunting knife or any other tool, used carelessly wrecks the turf.

As coinshooters we should carefully look at the problem of extracting items from the soil through the eyes of people responsible for the grounds we hunt. The groundskeepers have all sorts of problems, and coinshooters should not become another in a long list of troublespots. What can such folks think, when they see somebody probing and digging lawn surfaces they have long taken care of? Remember, people fear most that which they do not understand, and many busy caretakers simply do not know much about metal detectors and those who use them. They see probing and digging going on, and they often over-react before even trying to understand what is going on.

Look through their eyes, and be ready to talk with them, and explain exactly what you are doing and how. Don't lash back at them. Argument leads mostly to verbal or physical conflict, and such confrontations help neither the individual nor our hobby members. These caretakers have dealt with careless

littering, driving various vehicles across lawn surfaces, golfers too cheap to go to the green and indifferent to replacing divots, dogs and their endless
piles, and all sorts of pure-hellish vandalism. Here
you are, probing and digging, tools in hand, and
they want to know exactly what you are doing.

Be prepared to tell and show them, and be sin-
cerely friendly about it. It will win you more than
brownie points. You should wear that trash apron,
and hopefully when a caretaker shows up, have some
trash in it. Sympathize with their litter problems,
and mean it, for it is your problem, too! Show them
how a coin can be probed for and removed from grass
without scarring the surface. Let them know you
have no intentions of any vandalism, and that you are
only enjoying the area in your own particular way.
Stress that you will actually leave the area a better
place than when you came, through your dilligent
litter removal.

In small towns, and often in bigger ones, where
you wish to hunt parks, schoolyards, or church
yards, seek out the persons in charge. Mayor, coun-
cil member, principal, pastor, or qualified represen-
tatives of such leaders will greatly appreciate your
looking them up and asking permission. With such permission you can deftly parry the questions of any who
may ask what you are doing. You will gain for yourself in particular and the hobby field in general
great public relations. You will not find yourself looking back over shoulders wondering if someone isn't
about to tackle you verbally.

Good digging techniques are worth the trouble it
takes for one to develop them. Good coinshooters
should work dilligently to do so. It is good public
relations and it improves recovery. It insures continued access to good coinshooting sites, just as indifferent and careless digging ultimately bars such
access. Perhaps the best bonus of all is fewer marred
coins.

Add it all up. Good digging methods are a must.
Coinshooters, dig in, but make certain you do it
with tidy care!

TO DETECT BIG, THINK LITTLE

There are over three million acres in the U.S. The entire army of coinshooters, doubled, tripled, or quadrupled, could never entirely cover this vast area, let alone cover it well, not even if they worked dilligently, double-time each decent day of the week. Fortunately, no thinking coinshooter has to cover it all. One of the principal weaknesses shared by all too many detector users is the feeling that somehow they should cover it all, or as much as they possibly can. The truth is, bigger-better finds most often can be obtained by detecting smart, thinking small in terms of area.

Go to where the money is. Places where leisure, pleasure, and spending dictated the loss of money and valuables are places where a detector user can most probably find money and valuables. It may be fun to seek out-of-the-way spots, but many of these locations are not good coinshooting sites. Why? The poor inhabitant saved each cent, nickel, and dime, and spent or lost them at a nearby camp meeting, the circus or carnival that came by, or in some other congregating place where his or her usual care with hard-earned coinage was briefly dropped. Fun places were where poor people most often lost a coin or two, not around their meager homes.

These hot spots, these better-to-hunt places, these coin bonanzas are not usually vast in extent. The best of old parks usually has an area that is better, for some reason. Shade, windbreak, nearness to a concession, water or equipment. A churchyard may be loaded with items in one portion, hardly anything in the rest of it. Parts of a schoolground may have many good finds, whereas little can be found in the rest of it. A small part of a small place, when compared to the entire community, and yet that tiny fraction of the whole may be the very best hunting for many a mile.

This author wearies of the familiar woeful cry, "I just don't have any place to go coinshooting." My amiable reply, "ample heaps of bovine debris!" No where in the country is a would-be coinshooter too very far from some excellent spot to search. West, east, north, or south, no coinshooter is twenty miles from several metal-detecting spots worthy of attention.

What bogs most people down is that they realize how much ground they have not covered. Ask them about a specific place, and they will inform you that, "I hunted the place for several days a couple of years ago. I worked it out. I want somewhere new to hunt. I don't like to ask permission to hunt on private property."

Pinned down, these excuses often evaporate. "Hunted-out" spots sometimes prove to be Eldorados to a more persistent search. In haste, little was found. The person "covered" it, but didn't find much. No need to go back.

Think back to where YOU found the really old, better coins. Did you ever return to that spot, find other coins; in fact, do so time after time? Did you find these by going slower, carefully covering less area? Did you really begin to search carefully, to think small?

All this is very well, you may say, but does an active coinshooter keep ahead of his lust for good places and productive hunting if he must think small? If a site truly is small, it must eventually be largely worked out, given persistent attention. It may be true that no site ever gets entirely worked out, but some certainly approach that depleted status. Then, by necessity, must a coinshooter not proceed to less productive sites?

No, not at all. Most coinshooters never go past the going over and over of the same old places. They keep going back, finding fewer and fewer old items, more and more new stuff. This may be fine, if you do not mind finding the clad junk that passes for money these days, the cheap tokens we use in place of true coinage. To the person who truly seeks better material, this is not enough. It also is not necessary to stagnate upon that plane of hunting.

Most people suffer with a NOW syndrome. If it is not happening now, or happened within fairly recent times, these people simply do not see many things they would like to see. They go to today's parks, schoolgrounds, churchyards, and beaches. They never seem to think of the many yesterdays before them, of parks, schoolgrounds, churchyards, beaches, and other places important in yesteryears, now unused and forgotten. There are popular beaches of a hundred years ago that now are not as popular. Resorts, playgrounds, and popular areas of decades ago now often stand deserted. Overlooked, it can be added, by all too many coinshooters too busy complaining about no more places to hunt.

It cannot be the place of any author, any single article to sort out and list these tens of thousands of places around the country. The unfortunate truth is, should any given spot be named and praised in an article, often an unbelievable number of people then descend upon that spot. Alas, several things happen, then. Often, the folk who live at that spot don't like that much intrusion. Action to close the place to metal detecting sometimes takes place. Visitors find too many other visitors crowding the place, perhaps, and find very little there in their search, or even nothing at all. The author of the offending article may get irate, derogatory, and at times even threatening notes or letters.

The simple truth must be noted: YOU must find your own best spots. YOU must seek out better, older, and more rewarding places in which to use your electronic wand, your pass to hours of searching pleasure. YOU cannot expect to forever give yourself new and better places in which to hunt.

You don't like history? You don't like to read through that kind of junk? Too bad, there are pages and pages of local histories, most places, and they are loaded with clues as to the best spots to hunt. Old newspapers often tell of carnivals and circuses, ball games, church socials, community doings such as Fourth of July celebrations and parades commemorating this or that.

You have never sought out old maps? Never compared them with recent maps, never saw a difference between then and now? Again, too bad. The old maps are treasures in themselves, often giving YOU a clue to a private hunting ground. That old map, plus your personal knowledge, could easily pinpoint several good old locations, places you never thought of before.

You never have talked with older folks in the area you'd like to search? You don't like their mental wanderings, and they dwell on aches and pains, and better times gone by. Too bad, too bad. The older people know the things not written down, or things perhaps written down you haven't read or won't take the time to read. They know the now things of yesteryear, the play spots when they were young, or perhaps even the play spots of when their grandparents were young. Take some time to talk to the older ones. They enjoy talking, many of them, and you will be rewarded with knowledge often unobtainable elsewhere.

Towns boomed, and died. Silver City, Idaho as one example, had a population of about 3000 in 1866. In 1880 it's population was down to less than 600. Today, Silver City is the queen of Idaho's ghost towns, inhabited solely by those who spent time there in the summertimes in their cabins. 1865 and 1866 nickels were lost there, you may rest assured, in relatively small areas. Look up the values of dimes and quarters for the late sixties and early seventies, the glory days of Silver City. If it interests you, find a way of getting permission to hunt there.

You do not have to seek out ghost towns, however to find the old hot spots. Such sites abound in today's

cities, forgotten rectangles, triangles, and corners
that once resounded to games and laughter. Old
ballparks now oftentimes house commercial buildings,
the back and side areas of which can truly be rewarding. Old playgrounds, built upon, now come under
redevelopment, giving opportunities to coinshoot,
often over a rather wide timespan.

Such a sideyard can be a coin bonanza, long overlooked mostly ignored if not forgotten. Often junky,
discriminators can be most helpful. If a small area
is highly productive, the work of picking up lots of
trash becomes worthwhile. After all, small areas have
advantages. Magnets, discriminators, and persistence
can enable you to cover a small area, whereas a larger area would seem hopeless, and perhaps make you
give up.

Thinking small is not just for an area, it is also
for sounds. Too many coinshooters pay too much attention to the louder sounds. This, most of us know,
is too often tabs, etc. Those more feeble sounds are
the deeper coins, the older coins, for which you
should carefully probe. Those feeble sounds are what
most people ignore, or never hear in the first place
because of their undue haste to cover more ground.

Careful probing in conjunction with listening for
smaller sounds can be very rewarding. It saves a
great deal of digging. If you are careful, you need
scarcely ever   damage a coin, either. You can pinpoint its location by touch. Usually coins down to
five or six inches, and sometimes more, can be taken
out of a slit without even making a plug. If you must
make a plug, for deeper coins, KEEP IT SMALL
BUT DEEP, so there is less chance of the grass
dying. Then get all the dirt back into that hole before you return the plug and step on it to be sure
it is as far down as it can go.

Think small, coinshooter, in both area and sound.
Coins are small. Your time for hunting is too often
too small, so limit the area which you hope to cover
Small areas and small sounds will make for larger
recoveries, and better ones.

HUNTING THE "HUNTED-OUT" SPOTS

The pristine, virgin coinshooting sites are be-
coming fewer and fewer, as most detector-users
know all too well. Seldom does a person find an obvious hunting spot that has not been searched already, not anymore. To be sure, many private
house yards and privately-owned locations remain
still-untouched, but that is an entirely different subject. A subject worth much consideration and effort,
but not the same thing as working the often-hunted
sites. Who amongst us has not heard, over and over
again, "Oh, that's a hunted-out spot."?

Take me to it! Those "hunted-out" spots are not
hunted out. Often they are silver mines. Yes, some
places have become exceedingly thin. Coins in such
long, worked-over areas are scarcer and deeper.
After all, the old coins are not being replaced--no
more are being lost the government is not "wasting"
silver on common citizens anymore, and probably is
about to stop "wasting" copper on them, too.

The situation in "hunted-out" spots is interestlng,
and not dreadfully complicated. Most avid coinshooters
already realize this, but it is worth repeating. In
many places now, the detector user will find new
money, and with harder work, a few much older coins

The "easy" old material has been and is being removed. The obvious hunting sites have received a care- full going-over that has removed many coins, a fantastic bunch of junk, and last and most important , often has left a good many deeper, much harder to find coins. The looser the soil, the truer this is.

This article is not for you if you think the "hunt- ed-out" sites are easy. They are not easy places to hunt. They merely still have many old coins, targets that demand careful hunting. Such places demand of the hunter knowledge of good equipment and slow and careful search.

In these tough spots higher discrimination is usually not going to let you recover much more than newer coins and silver jewelry. It will cost you a gold ring now and then, even with some of the better detectors now coming onto the market. Too much discrimination spoils you, and it costs you depth and many of your best possible finds.

Failure to know how best to use your detector is going to cost you badly in this type of hunting. You will miss what it tells you, and soon you will say, "By golly, this place has been hunted out!" It probably has not been, not entirely; you just want things too easy. Learn your unit! Remember how long it took you to learn how to read. Learning how to fully use a detector is not much easier than that.

Haste will make hunting these places useless, too. One cannot hope to whip across a spot where the good old coins are deep with much probability of getting a signal.

The signals one has to listen for are small. Listen for that feeble but clear signal, for it speaks of deeper, older material. This is the very essence of hunting for older, deeper coins. It does take patience. You will have to sweep slowly over areas, often for stretches of time that test your patience, attend- ing to that low but firm response.

Even when you get that response, you don't have the coin. Do you carry a probe, preferably one that won't mar the coin? Fiberglass rods, brass rods, steel rods with a rounded ball brazed onto the tip will enable you to locate the coin without marring it.

After all, do you really want to get that 1916D dime or that 1877 Indian head cent out of the ground only to find you've scratched it? One scratch or more, big or small, a nick or a deep groove, you have cost yourself dearly. That thousand dollar dime suddenly is worth two hundred. Ouch, that does hurt.

Use the probe. It lets you know exactly where the coin is located, and without disturbing the soil much at all. Then use a good strong screwdriver to pry out the coin. Back off from the probe about an inch and a half. Carefully avoid the coin, push it down past the level of the coin, If the ground is hard-packed, you may have to do this two or three places so the coin can be forced easily to the surface. The screwdriver is the lever, you furnish the power, and that coin will come right to the top.

Do this right, and the soil will not be badly damaged, and grassroots will not be greatly harmed. Shove any loose dirt back into the ground, and step on the spot. Correctly done, the scar will be minimal, and there will not be a resultant brown spot.

Many cities have banned knives but permit probes. It is easier, often-times, to cut a plug to remove a coin, but this method has not been good for public relations. If the ground is too dry, the grass in the plug dies. If the plug is too shallow, the grass dies, and the plug probably gets pulled out.

Some jerk in Denver, several summers ago, and I hope he reads this and resents being called a jerk, went into Denver's City Park and cut hundreds of about inch-deep, eight inch diameter plugs. Naturally almost every one of them came out the first time the big rotary mower went over them. Prairie dogs would not have left the place looking much worse. Two other idiots, perhaps the same one and an added friend, used a posthole digger in Cheesman Park the year before that!

Here's a warning: I will go hunt up a policeman and take him to the site if I see such nonesense going on. It is absolutely unnecessary to do this sort of thing. If warning such people does not get a civil response, take firmer action. This is the sort of thing that will close down detecting for everyone.

Cutting a plug is sometimes the best way of getting out a coin. If you need to do so, try to avoid it during really dry conditions. Get all that dirt back in, and cut as small a plug as possible, with plenty of dirt on it. The grass will have a better chance of survival, and the area will be far less obvious if there is some die-back.

If this all sounds like hard work, it is. If it is too much, this sort of hunting is not for you. Nevertheless, it is not necessary to go off somewhere else to find good old coins. They are there in the "hunted-out park", the places you have about given up on hunting anymore. That is why the stranger comes in and amazes you with the material he or she found there. It was done by patient, careful searching.

It is always interesting to hear, "My, you were really lucky!" Yes, there is some luck attached to it. You do have to go right over that coin. The deeper the coin is in the soil, the truer that is. That's why the slow, painstaking search, listening for those minute signals. That's why the careful retrieval. That's why the conscientious digging, for you probably want to come back.

Remember to work out from where you get the better coins. Try to remember exactly where you find the best material. Do a bit of history search, and see why some spots are better than others. That can lead to finding even better spots.

If you are tired of grubby clad coins, learn to "hunt in little". You must pay more attention to the little sound. You must cover smaller areas. Do these things, and you will begin to find those overlooked Mercuries, those Barbers that have always been there The Seated Liberties will enter your recovery program and a whole tribe of Indian heads will yield themselves up to you. How about a herd of Buffalos? All these older coins are still to be found, often right there in the "hunted-out" spots in your own vicinity.

So get out there and hunt these spots that are "hunted-out". Lots of luck and good hunting!

DO THE UNUSUAL

In coinshooting, as in any human endeavor, do the unusual if you wish to do well.   Don't make the mistake of doing that which many others are obviously doing, or that which you have done long and often. Think a bit, and do things somewhat differently. Repetition of habits often brings diminishing returns, your habits or others' habits, when it comes to weilding the magic electronic wand.

Take an old ball diamond in a park, no longer used, but which you heard about somehow, and followed up.   You hunted carefully, and found some good old coins.   A good many old coins at first, in fact, one or two of which were real keepers with some numismatic value, and some silver that certainly is

worth saving up, these days. Excited, you keep
hunting the spot. You search carefully out from the
place, but in spite of coming up with a few more
coins, the finds steadily diminish. Finally it is a
rare find to come up with anything there. You hear
of another old park, one in which this or that person
has done fabulously well. You find the place, and
you may or may not find a single coin. You hear of
another such place, or maybe half a dozen, and
check them out with like results. Yes, you are
following worn-out habits: Yours, and even worse,
other peoples' worn-out habits. You are practicing
defeat, which is neither good for recoveries or self
confidence.

Switch, just a little bit. You like hunting old
ball game areas. Ask the old timers where such
games were played. Check some local history. Such
places may have one time or another been an open
field, and now still be an open city lot.

One friend did well at an old school. One area did
not prove productive. He found, by asking a few
questions, that the school ground had been leveled
in that unproductive area, and the dirt hauled away.
A few more questions told him where the dirt had
been hauled. By searching that dirt, coins were
found, and in a place where virtually nobody would
have ever looked.

Many people confine their hunting mostly to parks.
Too bad. Years ago many communities had no parks,
for such places were not common before the turn of
the century. Did that mean that folks did not congregate? Heavens, no, in pre-radio, pre-TV, pre-movies
days there was even greater desire to congregate than
there is today. There was many a popular grove, or
corner field, where gala picnics were held, and com-
petitive events such as ball games. Those sites are
often still groves and fields, too, and the coins once
lost there are in all probability still right there.
Such information is in many an old-timer's head, certainly in local histories, often on old city or area
maps, and many a good suggestion will be given to

any who'll just ask.

Ever hear of revival meetings? Chautauqua? Fourth of July celebrations? End of school events, often held in days of yore in some interesting spot at a distance calculated to enhance the sense of freedom amongst the long-suppressed students? Each of these places once was highly important. That importance during the intervening years has diminished but that fact does not take away the reality of those places and of the frolicking throngs that once lost valuables there. Look up the social events once held in your area. What a bonanza may await you should you take up this challenge.

Don't expect someone to come to you. The responsibility for this minor basic research is yours. Pursuing this sort of lead may well lead you into some clues of even larger caches, too, and it certainly will make you better prepared to do the more detailed legwork that sort of thing usually requires.

Check in the old area newspapers. Much is in those brittle pages. Perhaps it has been transferred to microfilm. Check them out, though.

As you see, doing something different in coinshooting doesn't mean wearing a neon-pink blazer festooned with blatant treasure hunting slogans, or adopting a pseudo-western drawl, or flaunting a veritable arsenal of the latest in detection equipment. I personally advocated a much quieter approach, and doubt that flamboyance ever really helped anyone truly interested in honest-to-goodness coinshooting of treasure hunting. Being different actually is something as simple as moving over into that vacant lot, once you've worked out that old site at the edge of the park, where many good old ball games once were played. Being different is nodding politely when you hear about that really terrific spot that has been so good to George or Pete or Sally, checking up on some clues of your own, and avoiding meeting eight different friends and acquaintances who are following up on that same great story you heard.

You have figured out, haven't you, that most great places mentioned often usually have been hunted rather carefully by those bragging about them?

It must be said, of course, that many a "worked-out" place is not worked out at all. Few places are ever entirely worked out. That is somewhat different than the topic at hand, however, and relates to hunting slowly and carefully for the deeper coins. That in itself is doing things differently, for most people do not hunt slowly or carefully, and all too seldom ever hear those fainter signals that speak of older, deeper targets. A few good coinshooters have taken this route of being different, and do well at it. They often do not realize the broader, greater potential they are missing.

A few people hunt bus stops. Have you ever checked out stops where the bus, trolley, or trains USED to stop? Try it sometime, but don't begin with the more obvious places. Others may have beaten you there. Coins were lost in this kind of place, yet these places are unsearched in many areas.

This is the sort of general suggestion possible in a brief article. Again, you have to dig up the specific information pertinent to you and your area. Think for a moment of what happens when a specific place is named in a national publication. It has happened, you know. That sort of pointing out specifics can mean hundreds of thousands of people descending upon a small area. That is how legendary tales get blown out of all reality. If this author mentions a specific place, and praises it, and you turn out to be the 1005th person to arrive there within a short time span, look at what is happening. I am promoting following bad habits, you are blindly following them. It does not make area residents happy, unless they take advantage of it as area merchants have done in the Lost Dutchman ballyhoo of the Superstitions. It would make readers unhappy with this author, even though the article were honest, sincere, and factual. The first arrivals might benefit, as might the 1005th, but in reality there is something absolutely ludicrous about a thousand five people driving to say some rural school yard because I mentioned that I found a good many Indian head cents there.

There is such a school yard out on the high plains of Colorado, and I did go there and do well. Mention it here, heck no, at least not by name. Find that sort of thing out for yourself! Believe it or not, that is the only practical, sensible way. You have school yards in your own area, and picnic spots, playing fields, and party grounds. You get the permission, you gain the access, and you reap the rewards of and bear the failures. That is the way this hobby works.

Yes, you will find plenty to work on. In fact, there will be plenty of priorities you must set. You will honestly find more to work on, if you dig much at all, than you will be able to do. Sort out all those clues. Some will be the sort that should be done NOW, perhaps because they are so interesting and promising, perhaps because if you don't do it NOW the chance will disappear. Some fall into a later category, and many, many are fine if you get around to it sometime off in the future.

Once you set your priorities, and have the best ones ready to go, DO them. Lack of drive keeps many a coinshooter from doing anywhere near what could be done. Simple fact: Most people think about doing things, and seldom get around to doing them.

Priorities are often seasonal. Winter often curtails activities, or enhances them, further south. Spring, with vegetation at its lowest, often presents the best opportunities to hunt certain places. Rainy weather can preclude searching some areas.

Concentrations of people have to be considered. You want to hunt where people have been, not where they are. The scene of a large summer outing would be impossible to hunt, but the day afterwards it reverts to a pasture, and the farmer probably will allow your hunting if you don't bother his cows. Early Sunday morning at a football stadium is like being alone on a desert isle when compared to Friday night or Saturday afternoon. Timing is everything for this factor.

In hunting urban renewal areas, again timing is important. You may not want to hunt with people still in the houses, but sometimes they don't leave

too far ahead of the bulldozers. That is why you often have to DO what you want to, because if you
hesitate, the chance may be gone. Many a good
spot has been asphalted, covered with a building, or
graded away or covered with fill. Don't wait, DO it.

   After you follow up on a few of these leads, you
develop, and have some success, nobody is going to
have to discourage you from going back to the same
old places and doing the same old things. Nothing
succeeds like success, and nothing is sweeter than
developing a good project and having excellent recov--
eries from it. There are still plenty of places with
old coins, and plenty of silver, if you do a bit of
homework, and that's a heck of a lot better than a
few clad coins sweetened only rarely by some old
goodie.

   Do be prepared to bomb out a few times. Some
leads take you to dead ends, some places have been
searched carefully by someone who thought of the
same thing earlier, and sometimes maybe your homework was insufficient or faulty. Go ahead, though,
and suddenly whole new coinshooting vistas will open
up to you. You will have success, and you will begin to wonder why you never thought of such simple
things before. You will find it easier and easier to
ask people questions. Where were. . .? Hello, I'm
_____. Would you mind if I hunted for some old
coins in your yard? Do you know where the. . .?
Everyone tells me you are the one to ask about. . .

   You will think of plenty of more questions to ask,
and you will find your own manner of doing so.

   Get out there and do something different from
what you have been doing, of following in the well-
trodden footsteps of the many others. Get off the
beaten path. Learn to hunt deeper, and pay more
attention to the barely audible. Develop better probing and extraction methods. Go on a reading binge.
Seek the wisdom and knowledge of those older folks;
learn to read maps.

   Be a little different! It's fun to hear people saying, "Wow, what a lucky person!"

THE BETTER COINSHOOTING FINDS,

A REMARKABLE INVESTMENT PACKAGE

To most metal detector owners the seeking after lost and hidden treasures, large and small, is virtually the beginning and end of the hobby. The old, rare, and uncommon object that comes up at times to all persistant hobbyists is far too often thrown casually into a box or a drawer and left there clanking around when it is occasionally gotten out to show friends or acquaintances. Too bad, too bad! An entirely different but related hobby field, and a potentially high-reward investment opportunity, is being too often overlooked by detector chasers around the country.

The plain truth is, some of the finds constantly being made around the country by hobbyist THers are worth a great deal of money. The sad part of it is that all too few of the finders appreciate or know how to turn such recoveries to the best advantage to themselves. The dollar value of such recoveries, often sold for a pittance, given away to mere acquaintances, damaged and lessened in value by unknowing mistreatment, and in various other ways lost to the finder is undoubtedly a mind-boggling sum. Nobody really knows the dollars and cents amount, but it is huge, doubt it not.

One does not have to be a numismatic expert as well as a coinshooter. It simply behooves chasers of the magic electronic wand to be aware of such things as key coins and historical oddities. A relic book or two and Yeoman's yearly Redbook are inexpensive research aids every avid coinshooter should buy if they are not available in a nearby library. A bit of looking can at times be worth a good many extra dollars. Looking through such books is a most worthwhile use of time that cannot actually be spent in actual coinshooting. Snowy and rainy weather can thereby be interesting and useful instead of frustratingly miserable.

A few examples of lost and gained investment possibilities are in order. Talk to other long-time coinshooters and many similar tales of woe and glee will promptly come to light. Some folks catch onto possibilities quickly, it takes most people various longer periods of time, and some persons never seem to catch on. The profit is there for all, nevertheless, if they are interested.

About twenty years ago I found a 1911S cent that would grade at least extremely fine. At that time it might have been worth a dollar, but a young neighbor was a coin collector going after her hobby hammer

and tongs. I gave her the II S for an eleven plain,
which I still have. The one I have may be worth
$10.00, the one I traded the girl is worth at least
$18.00. Not a great difference, and if that was the
only such poor trade I ever made, the tale would be
meaningless. As most other treasure seekers, however, that little story is only the beginning. The
point is, I gave away almost half of my potential profit, a high profit on something FOUND.

Anyone who finds something of value, remember,
has a very low base for their investment. The time
they put into finding such things is the most valuable part of such an investment, as a rule, and that
can really not be counted. Spending that time was
fun, and utterly worthwhile in itself. Any valuable
find, therefore, is gained at virtually a $0.0 base.
That makes potential profits rather fantastic.

Another example involves a friend who lived in
and hunted the parks of Longmont, Colorado. One
year, four or five years ago, he found two gold pieces.
One, a five dollar coin, found with a couple of
buffalo nickels, neither of which were valuable.
The other, a $2.50 piece, was no scarcity, but still
better than average in date and quality. He did not
need the money, but sold them to an acquaintance for
about the going price after some persistent wheedling.
That was not long before the spectacular rise in the
price of gold and gold coins. These past five years
or so have seen the value of those two coins at least
quadruple.

Needless to say, the man has not found another
gold coin since that time.

By keeping one's better coinshooting finds, unless
there is a financial need to sell them, a person can
actually use inflation to his advantage instead of always being the victim of it. Much of the rise in coin
values even seems to exceed the inflationary rise.
Few investment areas have much better track records.

I found an 1892 O half dollar in the sinful old silver camp of Cardinal, Colorado, several years ago.
The coin is almost uncirculated. At the time I could
not sell it for fifty dollars. Since then the Barber
half dollar series has seen spectacular price increases. This year I turned down several offers for the

An 1892 O 50¢ piece valued at nearly $1,000, among other coins and tokens. This coin was found in the foundation of a building at Old Cardinal Townsite below the ghost town of Caribou, west of Boulder, Colorado. About the middle of the picture below.

coin, the highest of which was for $225. That one half ounce piece of silver is indeed an excellent investment, as well as being a prize example of what can be found in ghost towns.

Mountain City yielded up another coin in almost as good a shape, an 1865 two cent piece. Mountain City, near Central City, was going strong in 1865. The coin was brand new when it was lost, or nearly so. A plaster wall fell onto the coin, protecting it over the decades since, when the houses were torn down and hauled away to other newer gold strikes because of scarce lumber.

The 1865 2¢ piece is now worth only $25 to $30, which brings up another point. That point is simply various types of coins experience cycles of popularity. During peaks of new popularity certain coins can have meteoric price increases. The 2¢ series has been long dormant, yet has a high scarcity factor. There is very likely to be renewed interest in the series eventually, and my single find could suddenly be worth many times what it is worth right now. That is the best kind of investment.

A good investment is bought at a reasonable price and is sold at a profit. The base price of coinshooting finds is usually quite reasonable. Profits of 100% are not uncommon over three, four, or five years, and that compares well with any investment. It compares far, far better when one stops to think that the 100% figure is obtained on what a coin was worth at the time of its finding, not its actual $0.0 base.

The best profits are not gotten through careless handling of one's finds. Cleaning techniques, methods of handling and storage, and how coins are stored all affect the eventual sales price. Two years ago, or more, a member of the Eureka treasure hunting club in Denver had the good fortune to come up with a 1918 D over 7 buffalo nickel, long lost in Denver's City Park. He had the misfortune to decide to clean it with an abrasive cleanser. Uncleaned, the coin would today be worth over $1000 at the very least. More, probably, for although the nickel was tarnished and grubby, as long-lost nickels usually are, it had rather sharp features. Proper cleaning by someone who knew what they were doing would have probably given him a coin worth over $1000 today. He was most chagrinned when he found what he'd done. He was also poorer if wiser. That was a most unusual and valuable find, and such a find should always be handled wisely and well until its value can be determined. The man had washed good money down the drain.

Most coinshooters have at times been guilty of throwing all sorts of coins into containers, irregardless of their potential value. It is foolish to do so, for there are various sorts of plastic holders available in which coins can be safely mounted. Scrapes, nicks, and rubbing can seriously detract from the eventual profits. Fingerprints and our often smoggy air is also often harmful. Many examples could be given of "could-be" valuable coins rattling around in boxes, handled and dropped by many people. We will allow the reader's imaginations to suffice. With a little thought, one can almost see the five and ten dollar bills disappearing in carelessly handled boxes of coins all around the country.

Removing the coins from the ground carelessly also removes potential profits. All of us have put scrapes and gouges on coins as we pulled them from the earth. What is really sad is to run a screwdriver or a knife blade right across the face of a truly rare coin. A mark like that has been known to subtract $500 from the coins value. I luckily have never had such an expensive slip, but I can show you a few itty-bitty scratches that have cost me $5.00 to $20.00. Careful digging techniques may become tiresome, perchance, but badly marred key coins are worse than tiresome.

To get the better coins one needs to search the more likely places. That sounds more difficult than it really is, for coins were used and lost from one end of the country to the other. There are, of course, better spots, and best spots. The coinshooter who takes the time to research and discover the best spots, pinpointing them as closely as possible, is the person with the best chance of finding many, many highly valuable coins. Less likely spots usually produce fewer, less valuable coins.

A group of sisters in Branford Conn. for instance have found a couple of Fugio cents by looking over a very specific area. Don Robinson, also of Branford, took a fistful of large cents out of one small area, and a good many other old coins as well, because he got permission to search one likely, if small area. An acquaintance of theirs, obtained permission in a nearby town to search an old, old campus came up with a veritable gold mine of old coins.

There is a town near Boulder, where there are no longer any buildings, that is a regular producer of 1914D pennies. Being near Denver, and a booming mining town in 1914, the place is well worth careful attention. The readers must forgive my failure to give the name of the place, but I am still enjoying the fruits of my research there. Look around you, there are manylikelyspots near you, no matter where you live!

One spot I feel certain to have an 1877 Indian head cent is King City, Colorado. That place also has little evidence left that it was once a boom town. King City produced coal between 1870 and early 1890's. Miners of coal were not rich, but they made good wages. They lost pennies, you may be sure, and those coins are still there.

Look around you. There are still many places to find good, old coins. Learn a bit about such coins, and perhaps consider them as much an investment possibility as a marvelous find. Just remember, we are only stewards of what we have. We will not take our finds with us, even if we want to, no more than did the one who dropped a coin into the dusty street of a town long dead. That is all the more reason to know something of the value of the objects you find, so that you may sell them at opportune times for your greatest profit. If you find it you should be the one to profit from your find.

OUT OF SIGHT, OUT OF MIND

"Out of sight, out of mind" is one old saying that pertains to treasure hunting thousands of times over. Anyone who seeks hidden treasures must always keep foremost in their mind a very simple, but most elusive fact: Someone who wanted to hide something valuable wanted it to be HIDDEN. It had to be in a spot that was not obvious, not easily blundered into, somewhere that resisted chance encounter. Entry could not be too difficult, unless it was a cache deliberately hidden away for a long term, for money probably would either be added or taken from the cache as need be. Whatever the spot chosen, in any case, the hider usually did his or her best to get it out of sight.

We will ignore that endless list of concealments outside the house, this time. Any house offers more places in which to hide things away than most people could ever imagine. No need to go out to the barn, sheds, or any of the other outbuildings this time, either. The house all by itself, is a challenge to a treasure hunter. There have been plenty of examples where long and dilligent searches, in houses where there was good reason to believe money was hidden, were not successful over long periods of time. When at last found, and many were never found, the spot was not impossibly difficult, it was just well out of sight.

Several years ago, Hunter Pritchard and myself found a nifty little trapdoor and a terrific little hidey hole. It was unfortunately empty, but it served as a good example of what a person wishing to keep something out of mind can do. The trapdoor was a section of the floor, every board cut slightly at random, to fit exactly. It had to be pried out.

The trapdoor was anything but obvious. It was beneath a removeable flour bin in the kitchen cabinet, and to see it we had to remove the flour bin. We would never have done it if we had not been closely examining the interior portions of the cabinet, another fine hiding place. (Bills often have been found thumbtacked or taped in such out-of-sight places, where they can easily be reached even though they are well out of everyone's view.) Below the trapdoor was a high and dry place in the crawl space, right up against a footing wall. Nothing was there, but we could see that objects had been stored there. What we know not, and your imagination is about as good as mine.

Such places can be found just about anywhere throughout a house. From the attic down through every room, and on down into the basement, cellar, or crawlspace, there are endless places in which valuables large and small can be hidden. Everything is not always what it seems at first glance to be. Double walls, false ceilings or floors, boxed-in places

LOOK HERE!

AN INTERESTING CACHE LOCATION

(In a house searched a few steps ahead of the house wreckers)

Here's the flourbins in the cupboards in the kitchen

Here's the trapdoor beneath the flourbins.
You'd never know it was there without
removing the flourbins

Here's the hidey-hole beneath the flourbins

between joists or rafters, hollowed beams, balus-
trades, steps, and who knows what all. It does not
take a place of great size in which to hide away a
dozen or so gold coins. Trim boards around windows
made to slide neatly out, have been found to hide
such small caches, caches made larger by today's
hideous inflation.

If you ever hope to successfully search houses,
learn to suspect spots hidden away betwen boards. If
it looks too thick, it may be too thick. Get out your
tape measure. Know the outer dimensions of a house,
and then find the inner measurements. You may be
looking right at a four foot room between walls and
not know it. Detectors are most helpful tools, but a
box of coins in such a place would probably be
missed unless it is right up against one wall or another. Only a partition wall may be between you and
a marvelous cache, in such a case. Such rooms were
built for a reason and what better reason for such a
place than someone's desire to hide away something
of great value?

Most people of yesteryear did not take time or
expense of building small, secret rooms into their
houses, but there were enough who created small
hiding spaces. Nobody really knows how many caches
were hidden away. Estimations have been made, some
by some really astute seekers after fortune. Whatever the answer might be, the number is fantastic.
Also, there is plenty being put quietly away today,
squirrelled away against harder times. We have no
more reason to trust policies and politicians than
our forefathers had. Your guess as to how much is
hidden across the country is as good as mine or
others. One thing, it is more than ever will be
found.

One estimation that seems as reasonable as others
is that one house in four has a hidden pocket of
money of some size or other. This could be a few
coins overlooked in some cranny to a multi-thousand-
dollar bundle tucked securely away. A crock in a
cellar wall, nearly full of trade tokens, might have
been worth many dollars. A jar of pennies might
have never been found by the heirs, even though
they knew of its existence, because a casual search

never dislodged it and a sale of the property pre-
cluded a more dilligent exploration.

Now don't get excited about every house, for you
won't be able to get to them all. Let's say you do
some research, decide one particular house may indeed have a potential cache. Money was unaccounted
for upon somebody's death, or some other valid reason makes you think a search is warranted. You
gain permission to search the place, or figure out
how to do so without interference. How do you do
it, and feel sure that you don't overlook anything?

Yes, use your detector, but remember that there
is and always has been a great deal of currency.
A detector is not going to pinpoint that, usually, and
a detector can never replace the mind. Your mind,
eyes, and judgment are usually better tools than a
detector. Work systematically. Develop your own
system.

You may decide to use your detector first. If so,
grid the place. It will help make sure you miss
nothing.

Searching takes patience. The three weeks of
searching by Sheriff Marvin Adams of Madison County, Nebraska, in 1971, and his deputy, Bernard
Staib, proves the necessity of patience clearly
enough. They knew that money was probably buried
though others had given up. They even knew that
the cache was in a basement. Even so, they were
about to give it up, after three weeks of meticulous
searching, in sheer frustration. Then, using a
steel probe, they banged it into the side of a metal
box hidden in the basement's dirt wall. There were
even other probe marks, where others had searched,
all around the actual spot.

How much can be found? Those two men were
able to return $53,200 to an estate where rightful
ownership could be determined. It was not old
money, nor was it too new. The point is, one man
who'd not been especially well-to-do had buried that
amount. Death had prevented his removing or using
it. It often happens that way. Sums well up into
the tens of thousands of dollars have been and are
being put away for various diverse reasons, and

most such bundles remain exactly where they are put.

Where are such tidy bundles? Would you believe in attics, in nooks and crannies of rooms, and in cellars, basements, and crawlspaces of houses? Do believe it, for they are there. Of course you'll not be able to poke and pry through most houses, but always remember that a cache remains even if a place is abandoned, in a decrepit to falling down stage, or even almost totally gone. Being often in some protected recess, a cache often remains intact even though the major portion a the house has disintegrated. Housewreckers are well aware of this fact, for some men in that field have found several such bonanzas merely by keeping their eyes open.

It is up to you, deciding just which houses to hunt. One thing, you'll not ever run out of possibilities. You can use a general shotgun approach, poking through any and all old run-down places you can get into. You can research, and find real money possibilities with particular old houses. You can even put research with a bit of rental money into a particular place, before it is abandoned or torn down.

The places to look, once in a house, are many. There are no absolutes, though, no places most prefered by those who hide money. In the hearthstone of the fireplace, behind the mantle, in the corner of a coalbin: None of these places are really THE place to look. Any place is the place to look, and all places. Sure as you pass over one spot, that may well be the place someone else discovers to be THE spot. Don't ignore the furniture, appliances, and other items inside the house. Remember that legs can be hollow, and that any enclosed volume can have unused corners in which things can be easily hidden. Large bundles of cash have been found stashed in odd corners of washers, table legs, false-bottomed bread boxes, and other common house furnishings.

Look over rafters, sills, and joists. Suspect every part of the house. A tin can nailed over a broken board may not have been tacked there to keep out mice, it may have been tacked there to look as though it was to keep out mice. A large bit sometimes was used to make a hole large enough to hold a certain size gold coin. The head of the right size bolt could be forced in the hole, with no bolt below it, with $2.50, $5.00, or $10 gold coins taking up the space. It is nifty little tricks such as that that keep a cache hidden a long, long time. Look things over, and look for things that seem fine at first glance, but somehow are just not right. Pipes that end too soon, too short a board, tin or some other covering over a hole, or boards tacked onto some place for no visble reason are good examples.

Look along the tops of rafters, trim boards, and other things up above eye level. It was easy to put objects on such places and get them out of sight. Single coins, guns, watches, rolls of currency, and rings have been found in such places extremely often.

Conversely, look beneath things. Under the base of trim boards, joists, and so forth. Anything that low is also well out of sight, yet easily retrieved. Objects are often found in such places.

There is money to be found. James "Silver Dollar Jim" West left a cache of about eight TONS of silver dollars in his basement when he died. A "pauper", Oscar Hastings lived in a filthy, ramshackle house, but left almost $100,000 strewn about the place after his death, in Columbus, Ohio. A dental technician, Michael Rorano, found in the basement of a Yonkers house he rented a lunch box containing $10,500. Two boys in Columbia, South Carolina found $2000 in twenty dollar bills. Where? Yep, under some bricks in a fireplace. A list of such publicized cache recoveries could be presented covering page after page, and totalling millions and millions of dollars. Reflect on the fact that fewer and fewer recoveries, for various reasons, are being reported.

Out of sight, out of mind is mighty good advice for today's THer, to heed most carefully. Report such a find to newspapers, and expect a deluge of crank letters, phone calls, and visits. You will be lucky to avoid lawsuits of one kind or another, wherein only the lawyers will profit. You will be bombarded with all sorts of plans for spending much of what you find, even if you get to keep any of it. Several who've recovered large sums of money have quietly paid taxes on any money they converted to their own use, not said a word about their finds to anybody, and have simply gone on about their business. There is a temptation to blab. The best advice possible is, DON'T.

House hunting, as in any form of treasure hunting, is often tiresome, dirty, dangerous, and absolutely frustrating. As with everything else, your success is improved manyfold by research. At the least, your chances for success are improved. The more and better the research, the greater the probability of recovery. If there is reason to believe there may be money hidden in one old house, that one old house is a better place to hunt than just any old house. That's a simple fact, but seemingly one that few would-be THers follow.

If you really think something may be there, search that one house from top to bottom. Don't overlook the obvious, for that may be just where what you seek is hidden.

Remember a few simple don'ts. Don't tresspass. Don't fail to get permission. Don't tear the place apart. Repair any damage you cause, don't leave it messed up, even though the place is either falling down or is to be torn down. Why advertise that you may have found something, or even that you were seriously looking. Don't talk about your search, let alone the success of your search.

Do keep your eyes open and your brain in gear. Do remember that what you seek was deliberately hidden. It was not meant to be visible. Ask yourself where you might have hidden something away in that house. Use your detector, but don't depend on it to the exclusion of real thought. Do have fun, for perhaps the adventure of the search in many ways is worth far more than any recovery you'll ever make!

TO FIND KEY COINS

LOOK IN KEY PLACES

Coins, like gold, are where you find them. Even so, some spots are much better places to seek those illusive metal discs than others, especially if you truly want to recover the more unusual, rarer, and most valuable coins. Key coins, the few that stand dollars and cents above other mintages. Giants in the pygmies of coinage.

Granted, any given key coin can perhaps be found almost anywhere. Out in the middle of a field, atop a rafter in an old barn, buried with others in a butter and egg money cache, in your grannie's attic. All sorts of oddball places could yield up a key coin, if the truth of the matter be known. One's chances of turning up the rarer, more valuable coinage, however, is dramatically increased by judicious selection of where one hunts.

The 1877 Indian head cent comes to mind at once in such a discussion. It is the most valuable penny in the Indian head series, the most sought-after of that group by collectors, and the toughest to come by. There were only 852,500 of this particular coin minted, and such a few scattered over an immense land doesn't stretch too far. What to do, being both coinshooter and either coin collector or desirous of selling that coin to a collector? Hope? Pray? Await your chances, and see what comes up? One in good condition sell for about $90. In extra find condition it sells for over $400. Should you be lucky enough to find one in a cache, in uncirculated condition, it should bring you over $800. Uncirculated coins which coinshooters seldom encounter in coins long lost in the soil, are worth most often about double or better the next step down, extra fine.

The 1877 cent is a marvelous find. How can one ever hope to find one? There were admittedly very few of them struck! What hope does a person have of ever encountering one in any shape or condition? The answer is not simple, for the 1877 is truly a rare coin. The best way to go about it, however, is to find a place where there is a better than average chance for such a coin to be.

The idea is to find a spot that was booming at the time the coin was issued, and continued to go strong for at least a while afterwards. Boom towns often had hard cash when it was dear elsewhere. 1877 was a hard year, yet there were places where men were paid in cold coin for hard work. Such boomtowns saw hard working, hard drinking, and wild living. Such scenes saw a good deal of money lost. Fights in the streets, drunks tossed out of bars into muddy streets and so on.

Such a town was Garland City, Colorado. It was a railhead city in 1877 and 1878. There was nothing there before, and there has been nothing there since. Yet in those two·years several thousand souls lived fast and hard there. You may rest assured that many an 1877 cent hit the dust, and that is still where it is. The townsite is not too hard to find. It is east of present Fort Garland, and the graded roads of a would-be subdivision through and close by. You could probably buy much of what was the very heart of the place for not too vast a sum. The development company would be happy.

You can and should figure out sites equally as good, and very likely much closer to your own home. The idea is simply to put a rare date coin with an accessible townsite that was thriving at the time a coin was issued. If the spot is near the location of the mint, so much the better. Nevada Ghost Towns are one of the very best places to search for the rare Carson City mints, for instance. Louisiana is a logical place to more likely find some of the hard-to-get New Orleans mint coins. Figure it out for yourself, and act. The examples given here are only meant to serve as aides in YOUR thought process. Don't ten thousand readers run right out there, for heavens sake! Pennies are the most commonly lost coins, and therefore the most commonly found. People have never been quite as careful with them, and they certainly are not careful with them these days. Fortunately for coinshootersthere was little extra care taken with even the rare-date coins. They were lost right along with the other pennies. Not as many are found for the obvious reason that mintages were extremely low. That is the main reason a coin is scarce.

Another scarce date cent in the 1914D. It is now valued at more than $35.00 on up to over $150.00. More in uncirculated condition, of course.

In 1914 the town of Tungsten was a rip-snorting place. The price of tungsten was high and a rich ore body of the useful-in-alloying-steel metal had been tapped just east of Nederland, Colorado. About 9000 people soon crowded into the confines of a narrow valley. The mines thrived, money flowed, and many, many rolls of new cents surely were sent up from the nearby Denver mint.

About a third of the site is now under the waters of the lake formed by Barker Dam, and much of the rest was disturbed by construction during the building of the dam, but there's plenty of space left. Nine thousand people leave plenty of traces, and a few coins, too, when one really starts looking.

A place does not have to be large in order to be a worthwhile spot to search. I missed finding the 1885V nickel, the most valuable one of the series, by one year. I found an 1886, worth only $28.00 instead of about $60.00 the 1885 would bring in good condition. I would not sell it for many times that, for something else enters the picture. Where the coin is found often adds value to the finder all out of proportion to the actual numismatic value of the find.

I found three liberty head or V nickels outside of an old dugout saloon in Bridgeport, Utah. A friend found a Rock Springs, Wyoming dollar trade token there, too. Bridgeport, right in the middle of Brown' Hole was frequented by Butch Cassidy and his Wild Bunch.

Uncle Jim Nicholls showed me the place, or I'd never have found it. He is now dead, but when he was 18, and working on a new irrigation canal being built in that valley, he drank beers in that tiny saloon and well remembered listening to a couple of the Wild Bunch spout off about their escapades. The nickels were probably dropped by the saloon keeper, but I like to think that one of Butch's cronies just might have handed it to him for a beer. I would not take several times that coin's $28.00 current value. Would you?

Everyone familiar with coins knows the value of 1921 coins, especially those from the Denver mint. The 1921D half dollar is now worth $350, extra fine. In that condition the 1921S is worth $450, though not worth as much as the Denver coin in good or very good condition. The plain 1921 is worth from $35 to $310. The 1921 quarter is valued at $25 to $95, good to extra fine. The 1921 and 1921D dimes are similarly valuable. Any coinshooter would like to find any one of these precious silver coins.

1921 was a slack year. That's why the low mintages that now make those particular coins worth many dollars. Some spots that were not completely slack at that time were the coal camps of northern New Mexicc and southern Colorado. The miners there were not rich, but they were drawing good wages. Dawson, Koehler, and Brilliant, in the Raton area, and Tobasco, Hastings, and Segundo in the Trinidad area are only some among many towns with populations well into the thousands each where some of these coins were undoubetdly dropped, left and forgotten. To all except enterprising coinshooters, of course.

Remember, just attach a going place to a key date coin, and you probably have a chance of finding that coin there. Money gravitates to where economic activity is in full swing. If coal is being mined and sold, no matter how hard times are elsewhere, there is money there. Ditto lumber, cattle, farming, construction, and on and on down through the long lists of human endeavor.

There are several factors that go into determining what makes a key coin,"key"meaning vital to completing a collection of a particular series of coins. The most important, of course, is the total mintage. The truly rare key date coins are what coinshooters dream of finding. Virtually none of some issues are in coin collections. They all disappeared into circulation. Some were put away in a cache, be it post hole bank or box in the trunk in the attic, and some were lost. None simply vanished from the earth although some melted down in fires and such accidental changes or mutilations. That is why rare, extremely valuable coins can be and are being found.

Some key coins had fair-sized mintages, yet are rare today because of being out into circulation before anyone had any idea they were going to be rare. A recent example of a key date coin is the 1970D half dollar. All of these particular coins came out in a limited mint set mintage. There were none at all released for circulation, and the price and scarcity factors are high. Things of that sort happened more regularly and with far greater finality years ago, for there were few coin collectors, and virtually no long-range coin speculation as there is today.

It is worth knowing about the key coins. Get a good coin guide, or several, and a grading book. You cannot easily be aware of the value of the coins you find, otherwise, without having someone examine them. Most coins found in the ground cannot be called truly uncirculated, though some dealers now would sell them as such, even though they purchase them from you at far lower prices. Knowledge is important to you in getting the best possible prices should you decide to sell your coins.

Most keep-at-it coinshooters find a good many of the coins worth ten to one hundred dollars. Gold coins are harder to come by, but they are being found, too.

The extremely valuable coins are worth many hours of searching. The very possibility of finding a coin valued in the thousands of dollars is what keeps many a coinshooter drooling after his zig-zag-ging magic wand, for the chance of finding such a coin is ALWAYS there.

The fact remains, you are most apt to come up with a key date coin if you go where the probabilities of doing so are greatest. That demands research as well as careful search. That all-important word, research, so few THers really take the time to do it. You need to develop research skills. When you do put key-date coins with logical spots for such coins being lost, your chances of recovering them improve. You still may not find what you seek, but what you find will be older and better if you do find anything at all. It is not blind luck, this coinshooting, or it need not be. The 'lucky' person thinks, then acts, whether he or she stops to analyze what they do or not. They may not sit down and write out a plan, but successful people do have one.

So dig into your basic local facts, Coinshooters. Do it if you want to find valuable coins. Know where people were when they had those key coins in hand, and never prized them at all except as hard-earned money, and you may find where a few of them were lost. One such find would seem like a fairy tale come true. Bypass the leprechauns and other lucky charms. Use your head and your detector correctly, and you may find your pot of gold at the end of the rainbow in a single coin. You may be digging close to me out there, too, so even if it's a good one, fill in the hole!

FOLLOWING PATTERNS

Most vocations and avocations follow patterns, and to do your best in coinshooting, you must be able to follow the patterns others have set. A few coinshooters already know this. Some coinshooters know it to a degree, or at least practice many of the skills inherent in that knowledge without fully realizing it. Too many people, however, who'd like to improve their coinshooting abilities, have never given enough thought to this idea of finding and following patterns, let alone allow it to help their hunting.

Patterns followed over a period of time can be traced, often many years later, once the tracer figures out the pattern. Archaelogists have made a science of this, and increasingly use it in their labor. Coinshooters can multiply their effectiveness manyfold by doing the same sort of thing.

A few examples are in order.

Sidelines of football, and other ball games, are often most productive of coins. Knowing this, try to find out where games of yore were played, and the types of games once played there. How? Ask old timers, look at old city maps, read some local history. It's simple, basic research. Locate the spot, then prospect, just as a gold-seeker must do. Remember that bushes or trees might not have always been where they now stand. Find a few coins, see if they run in a somewhat straight line, then really go to work. Act as though that playing area is still there even though there is no sign of it,and follow those once-upon-a-time sidelines.Work out from that pattern,of course.If you find a concentration of coins,ask yourself why they might be there. Was it near home plate? Was it a sideline? Was it where onlookers must have sat, watching the game?

Not all patterns were formed in city parks and school yards. Therefore, don't confine your hunting to those places.

Parking meters, both those there now and those that once were there are worth searching around,

Follow patterns.

Young people lay around, visiting, sun-bathing at Colo. Univ. in Boulder, Colo.

or in a city park.

or at a beach.

or at the football stadium.

especially if the area around them has never been paved. That is an easy to see, easy to follow pattern. So is any parking, or that strip between the street and the sidewalk. Many people have long and productively worked these parkings. Follow along sidewalks and paths, especially where they near small stores. Such paths near schools can be silver mines. Have you ever thought about working paths that were once there, that led to stores that were once there, but both now gone? Such information is not all that hard to uncover.

A good clue, if you've not used it, is that people sit around trees and lose change. So what, you ask. Have you ever looked around where trees used to be, in parks? That's where the older coins are more easily found, and that is certainly following an old pattern. Seek out those slight depressions and old wood chips that are a giveaway that once a big tree stood there.

Another pattern has been mentioned elsewhere, but is worth repeating. In the immediate area of rural mailboxes, many coins can often be found. Over the years, change was left in the mailbox, for stamps, postage due, and so forth. Some of it got knocked onto the ground, and not all of it was picked up. Can you imagine how many miles of mailboxes there are in this country?

You surely have looked for old swimming holes. They are some of the best hunting areas of all. In many cases ponds have gone dry, but the coins are still there. Find the pattern of where people undressed and sunbathed, and you will find coins, even if the lake has been dry for years.

Ghost towns. Again, find the streets, the paths, the gathering places, and you will find the largest number of lost coins. Find the doorsteps of the houses.

One's search benefits when he or she figures out the patterns of activity that made for greater coin or jewelry loss. An old lovers' lane, even if it is now a cornfield, some empty city lots, or a school yard, can well yield some coins and jewelry. Knowing the direction of that lovers' lane and being able to follow it in spite of present use means more recovery.

Follow old bus routes, and find where popular stops were before the route changed. Hundreds of coins can be found in such places. Old trolley or streetcar lines, the same. Ditto old railroad depot areas. People may have stopped waiting for the train years ago, but the coins they lost before they stopped waiting are still there, unless someone else has already figured out that pattern.

Money exchanged hands at ferry crossings, canal depots, stagecoach stops, and excursion terminals of all kinds in years gone by. Too often, today, we tend to never think of such things. We don't have those things now, so most people never even think of such activities.

Where were the old picnics, holiday celebrations, bandstands, rallies, and parades of yesteryear? Almost every town at one time had a yearly carnival, often over many years. Those can be marvelous coinshooting sites, especially where there were coin pitches and concession stands.

Try the old revival sites, especially if you can find out where the main meeting sites were. Offerings were taken, and all the coins did not always get into the plates. Sawdust floors, or just out on the grass, many a coin got trampled into the ground.

Have you ever watched fireworks displays? So have many thousands of other people. If you can discover where people sat to watch such displays over the years, especially if the site is no longer used, that is coin country.

These patterns have similarities, but all of them have their differences, too. Who played on the ball fields, for instance. Younger children lost pennies perhaps, whereas college kids and young adults lost the quarters and halves. Maybe a good ring or two. When were the games played? If they were played at night, or in wet weather there is a better chance of lost items not being found. Who would play in wet weather? Well, football players often get snowed on, and baseball players have been known to get rained out.

Proximity to some place that sells things often is important. People tend to have less money where there is no chance to buy things. That hotdog stand, that corner market, a nearby ice cream parlor, or any other dispenser of goodies around a play area often means lost money. One loses money if they have money to lose.

Are there ski lifts in your area? Look mainly where people get on and get off, or where they stand before going downhill or gain their breath after coming down hill. Look at the base of hills where sledding has gone on for years, or where innertubing is now occurring. The top of that hill, and all in between is not quite as good, but still worth a good search.

Is there a place where gambling went on, or where drunks slept it off?

Patterns developed in given places according to what went on there. In a fishing village, find out where the men sat mending nets over the years, but better yet, find out where they drank. Saloons are good almost anywhere, and that is most true in boom situations. Logging, mining, construction: Almost any type of expansion situation. Wild times breed feverish activity and carelessness. Where death was common, many small cache was never reclaimed. Fighting and drunkenness left many a good coin lost in a dusty or muddy street. Diseases we no longer fear wiped out many a families' hope and finances, years ago, because the one who buried the wealth died without telling where. Learn some of the money cache patterns, and sooner or later you well may come across a good one. It will increase your probability of finding one if it won't guarantee it.

Patterns. We use patterns to make things, to build things, and to guide whole systems. Is coin-shooting any different? Work at discovering the patterns that went into the makeup of your area, and you will astonish yourself in better coin recovery. People do, and they always have done most things in surprisingly set patterns. Attune your thinking to one of these old patterns, and increase your finds.

RECONSTRUCTING THE PAST

Sooner or later most seekers after treasure come face to face with meager traces of places and events long gone. They stand there with very little to see around them. They know, because they were told, or they researched on maps or in the written word, that such and such was right where they stand. They find, however, it most hard to believe that any thing was ever there.

Impatience, laziness, and a lack of understanding of what to do next brings many THers to a total, frustrated halt. They grumble, and soon leave what probably is a very worthwhile hunting area. They never return. They give up ghost towning, search-ing for old carnival and recreation sites, and prob-ing abandoned dwelling places as a lost cause. Too bad for them, for there are ways of making the searching of such spots somewhat easier. Not effort-less, mind you, for soil erosion and deposition, plant overgrowth, and the many other fine-grinding teeth of time successfully hide almost everything that man leaves behind.

Even with old maps, old pictures, the careful description of old timers, and a good imagination, a search of a bare-bones site can be difficult. Many a site has scarcely a depression, a foundation stone, or any other indication that man was once there, at least not at first sight. Don't believe what you see in such cases. Men did indeed live there, and they hid and lost many things that are well worth search-ing long and hard for. Too, the less obvious things are, the more likely that place has not been searched well if at all. Don't give up before you begin. Learn to reconstruct the past. Then, especially if you have the help of various descriptions, maps, and pictures, you should be able to do very well in-deed. Even without such aids it is often surprising how well one can flush out the ghosts of that which once was, at least well enough to see where things were.

The purpose of this is to point out obvious and less than obvious indicators of the past. Most folks walk right over such indicators without seeing them. THers cannot afford to do that if they hope to re-cover much of anything. Therefore, learn to fill in those gaps, and you're well on the way to improved coinshooting. Treasure hunting is full of the most frustrating of gaps, and learning how to go around, go across, or fill in such missing information is what our hobby is all about. Those who do learn how to do this are those we label "professionals".

Realize that the small, isolated spot, far out in the boonies, is not always the best place to search. Most of us have been guilty of seeking out such places, and usually have bypassed dozens of better sites while going there. Consider: Most such places were not the haunts of successful outlaws, miserly hermits, or moonshiners, but only the homes of frugal inhabitants living poorly on the thin edge of poverty. Most of them had very little money. They lost very little of what they did have. They had to spend their money, not cache or lose it. Therefore, a more realistic approach is to seek out the less isolated spots. The exception is when you are going afer the successful outlaws, the miserly hermits, or the moonshiners--or another of such ilk.

For instance, the successful farm of today is often atop the successful farm of yesterday. Find the old house sites, and you will find old coins. The same goes for old towns, now built over by larger towns or cities. Learn where the old part of town was, and you will probably find old coins. Learn how to ask for permission to search yards. That is a prerequisite to successful town and city searching. You will give yourself all sorts of trouble and the hobby field in general a bad name by sneaking onto spots where often you could get permission to search with little effort.

Look for unatural variations in the surface level of the land. If it is lower or higher for no natural cause you may be sure it is the fault of man. Such visible places should be checked carefully for debris. Ditches were often made around buildings, and it takes a long time for such depressions to completely disappear, even in a plowed field.

Speaking of plowed fields, go back to sites after new plowings once you locate a good place. New plowings bring up items that were below detection range. This happens year after year. Go when nothing is planted, and get that permission.

Look carefully at the trash scattered on the surface of any given site. Debris can tell you many things about a place before you ever take out your detector. What makes up the debris? Is it glass, pottery, brick, rusted metal, wood chips, or just exactly what do you find?Where do the traces start, and where do they end?

Back east, near the shores, bits of seashell can often be found in with the fractured bits and pieces that show people once lived there. No foundation may mark the spot--indeed, it may be in the middle of a plowed field.

In flat land, long-farmed, search for areas covered with various scattered debris. The more of it, the longer a given place was occupied, and the more chance there will be of finding lost coins and artifacts. Different times different areas made for a different composition of debris. This is most helpful in figuring out what sort of a site you've found. The older it is the less rusty iron there will be. We live in an age when we take for granted iron and steel. It is the backbone of our civilization, and much of it is discarded, scattered. Not so, in earlier days. Iron was far more expensive and harder to come by in the early days of our country. Bits and pieces were picked up to re-use. Also, there has been more time for iron to rust away, if any was discarded, in the older areas. Learn something of old glass, pottery, and brick making, for traces of these things make very obvious the age of a site. As tab tops indicate recency, many old crockery shards indicate a time long gone. Such are the tiny but important arrows pointing to lost coins and artifacts.

Search for areas having much decomposed wood. The old wood piles were littered with sawdust, chips and small bits of wood. This material may decompose but it takes centuries for it not to be noticeable in the soil. It will often make the texture and color of soil stand out from the soils around it like a sore

thumb. Near this woodpile stood the house. Realize that usually the woodpile was toward the rear of the house, or off to one side or the other, hardly ever out front, so by that alone you can estimate more or less where the structure stood.

Also seek out the ash piles. They, too stand out from surrounding soils. Learn to tell wood ashes from coal ashes. Here, too, the more burnt, rusted iron there is in the ashes, usually, the newer the site is. Widespread use of coal is more recent. Wood cost only a lot of labor, coal cost money, which was hard, hard to come by for most people in the early days. Bits of coal and coal ashes may indicate a family that had relatively more money.

Wherever you look, watch for depressions, however small, and any unnaturally flat spots. Any such obviously geometrical area is a sign of human activity. Many of the ghost mining towns, for instance, had much the same layouts, usually limited by the topography of where they were located. Many a mining town was cramped along the bottom of a steep-walled gulch. Visit Creede, Colorado, some time. Space was at a premium, flat areas were not large or they eventually washed away. People then knew that but often had to build there anyway. Too far up the slope brought problems with climbing up and down and increased the dangers of being caught in rock-slides, snowslides, mudslides, and similar fates. Look for terraced spots in such areas, for there stood the buildings.

Life was a good deal different in the communities of yesteryear than it is in our towns of today. No TV, no radio, no picture shows; none of the many recreational conveniences we take so much for granted these days. Work hours were longer. It was nice if there was time to sit out on the porch and talk or read a newspaper or perhaps just sit. The weather did not permit it all too often. Find where the porch was, for a good many coins can often be found in a very few feet. In bad weather, people often remained indoors. This is a fact coinshooters should know. There were often large cracks in the floorboards of the little-better than shacks, and many coins have been found inside the foundation area.

Finding old fence lines can be of great help in determining how and where things were located. The job is not impossible either. Shovel and a steel probe are the required tools. Even though the posts are long gone above ground, the bases of wooden posts have left their decomposed remnants Locate a couple of these holes with probe and shovel, do a bit of eyeballing, to get the line, and soon the old yards, barnyards property lines, and whatever else the fences separated will become known to you.

The steel probe will also be most useful in locating outhouse pits and trash dumps. It also helps pinpoint the edges of large, deep artifacts, which can save much digging.

Vegetation can be a great aid in determining what was where. Larger, lusher growths often indicate outhouse pits, hen coops, hogpens, old septic tanks, overgrown wells, barnyards, and many other such items. If the same kinds of plants in a certain area are much larger and healthier than those about them, and especially if there is some geometrical pattern to the growth, it is often the clue to how a place was laid out. Also this is true if vegetation is less healthy. There may be some reason. Plaster is not exactly the best soil conditioner. It can retard plant growth for many years. Other substances can be as bad, or worse.

An old tree, or a group of trees, and especially a a line of trees is a good indicator of a former house place. The drier an area, the more true this statement becomes. If trees, living or dead, are out there all by themselves it is very probable that someone lived beside them.If you go there and find old bushes and tightly grown flower clumps, whether there is an old foundation or not, you are at an abandoned house place.

There are many clues to help one reconstruct the past. They vary from area to area, from seacoast to interior, from plains to mountains, from timberland to desert. One must develop an eye especially for the area in which he hunts. It is hoped these words will be of some encouragement in doing just that. It is up to you, so get out and find the old places others have overlooked. Your recovery of old coins and artifacts will improve!

LEARN YOUR OWN SOIL CONDITIONS

One of the most badly misunderstood problems faced by coinshooters is how best to search the very ground upon which we walk. The stuff is not just dirt. The other day, in Dallas, several friends and I were discussing this vexing problem, and Roy Krupa asked me why I didn't do up an article on the subject. After all, he suggested, everyone needs to consider the problem more carefully.

For that reason, I'm going into it. At the risk of smudged clothing, dirty hands, and filthy shoes, the subject is SOILS. The I & I Treasure Club does not call its newsletter The Dirty Five for nothing.

Soil is not simply the stuff upon which we walk. It is made up of many different elements and affected by all sorts of things. Too much of and not enough of various substances make soil in one place far different than the soil elsewhere.

Knowing one's own area soil, of course, is of importance to a coinshooter. Those soils affect the detector use. A different type of soil will make a detector react in a different manner. One can get different readings by moving over a few feet at times, and many beginners often think that something is the matter with their machines. No so. It is the dirt.

This subject is not geared to high suspense and tight fascination. Still, the facts are worth knowing. Dirt is composed of definite materials, so let us mention the reasons that soils in different places can be so incredibly different. Humus, or decayed vegetable and animal materials, clay, and sand, of sizes from very small to extremely large, or some combination of these materials, make up soil. The results differ from place to place, and from the surface down to bedrock. Naturally it is not quite that simple.

Other elements and compounds enter the picture. There are almost a hundred elements, which are not often totally "pure", and thousands of compounds, or unions of these elements. No, you don't need to go back and review your basic chemistry, elementary geology, and progress into an advanced soil sciences class at a good agricultural college. You only need to know that differences do exist and that they do affect the performance of your detector.

Some soils have very little mineralization, or substances which lessen the effectiveness of the detector's use. This type of soil is lovely coinshooting, and if you live there, lucky you. Other soils do have metallics, salts, and other substances that curtail the message the detector is built to give you.

You expect to get a signal if you pass a loop over a piece of sheet metal. Solid iron makes the detector react. Nature has broadcast iron, bauxite or other allumina, and other metals, in billions of small particles. Very few soils are completely free of such particles. What we call mineralized soils just has more of them. Various salts are also to be found in some soils. Try seashores, or lakebeds subject to periodic filling and evaporation cycles.

Many salt-affected soils affect detection through a mineralization almost opposite to the mineralization caused by metalics. Some writers have called this a negative and a positive mineralization, and that seems to be a good enough terminology. It does mean that your detector may work on the beach, and not in the mountains, or vice versa.

So, back to point one. Learn what YOUR soil is, and how to work it. Don't worry about the next county or state over, worry about what YOU have to contend with. You may not have to fight a negative mineralization, or your soil may not be positive.

A good, rich humus is probably the best soil, especially when there is some moisture in it. Less mineralization is present, and objects can be found at deeper levels. Humus is not all decayed material. There is some sand and some clay, hopefully in rather balanced amounts. When more gravel than sand is present, the mineralization usually is greater. Too much clay, digging becomes a severe problem outside of a few days a year. Too much water in clay soils and you get muck, slimey to almost obscenely gooey. Too much plant material, the soil becomes acidic, and those conditions can begin to reduce detection in a manner similar to that found upon the seashore. A very sandy soil can give all sorts of problems, mineralization-wise.

The object is to find out what you normally have to contend with. Digging tools for very sandy soil are not the same as for heavy clays. A plug can be cut deeply and neatly in damp clay soils, with little harm. In loose, sandy soil plugging does not work at all well, a screwdriver, well-used, works far better in removing the objects of your search. Tuning on the same unit will be different in different spots, and there is no one answer to put down. Careful experimentation is the very best way of finding out what your instrument is capable of doing in a given area. Probing can be highly rewarding in many soils. Too much gravel, and you might as well not try to use a slender probe.

Run a magnet through the dirt in your area. Often times, in fact in most places, you will pick up a heavy coating of black sands, a form of iron. It is a very common element, iron, upon this earth, and very much of it cuts down most detectors' efficiency in a hurry, or demands knowing and careful tuning and detector use. Salts upon the beach sands, too, make the detector act up. Wet salts are different than dry salts, you may have noticed.

You may be expecting to run your unit without

much sound. Good luck. Usually a unit should not be run silently. Sensitivity is cut down when "that noise is tuned out". Tune up the sound and see if you don't get better results.

A few generalizations concerning soils may be helpful, although there is no way of entirely covering everything in any short discussion. The regolith, or parent material, is what determines the soil. In places where glacial drift covers the land, that is the parent material, not the bedrock under that. The same is true of lava flows and other volcanic material overlying an original surface. This regolith breaks down into soils through the processes of decomposition, or chemical weathering, and mechanical disintegration.

The depth of soils varies. It can be as much or more than eighty feet deep in the tropics. In cold climates it is much shallower. In deserts there is often very shallow soil, and sometimes none, for in such harsh conditions wind and water often remove it as fast as it breaks down.

Humus, or organic materials, turn soils dark and soft. Very black soils are often not only very fertile, they also have lesser amounts of materials that adversely affect metal detectors. Grasslands actually add more humus to soils than other vegetation zones, for the grass roots decay within the soil. Leaves decay on top of it, and are often blown or washed away to a large extent. Earthworms and other burrowing creatures are most active in the better soils, thriving upon decaying vegetative materials within the soil. Therefore, even though the soils offer little amounts of heavy mineralization, coins are often far deeper. Whereas in the desert a coin may be only a bit below the surface, though lost a hundred years ago, the same coin in a rich soil area may be a foot or more below the surface, if lost that long ago.

One begins to get the idea that things often even themselves out.

Coniferous forests especially make for acidic soils. This makes detection somewhat harder, and often does very nasty things to coins lost there.

You cannot choose your soil conditions, so you'd best learn how best to work them. Oftentimes the best coinshooting is in a place where there is lousy soil. Get the detector that best solves the problem, learn exactly what it will do, and you will make other coinshooters say, "That guy is surely lucky. He finds all sorts of coins in that terrible soil he has a-round where he lives. I can't hardly find a thing there, yet look at all the stuff he keeps coming up with. He must be a wizard."

No wizard, you will have just learned what your detector will do in the soils of your area. Get out there, experiment, observe, and dig up more coins!

A STATE OF MIND

Different people seek different things, and for different reasons, but it all comes down to the thrill of the search. Coinshooters, numismatists, relic collectors, stamp collectors, and camera bugs all have one thing in common: They seek the hidden, the difficult to obtain. One who takes up today's detectors and seeks the lost and hidden valuables of yesteryear is really seeking adventure, freedom from a smothering governmental/bureaucratic morass that seems to become ever more stifling. It is this seeker's hope that drives him on, through and over all sorts of problems, his state of mind.

A true coinshooter KNOWS there are plenty of things to be found with his electronic magic wand. That knowledge enables him to face the scoffs of non-believers, find at least some of what he seeks, and pursue a growing way of life in spite of the many who think him foolish. The wise coinshooter will not even attempt to dissuade the scoffers. By showing what he finds he arouses envy, covetousness, and a host of other such baser human emotions. Comparing notes with friends and like-minded people is one thing, howling success to the world is another. If the coinshooter KNOWS what can be accomplished, is there really a need to convert the skeptics? Long-time seekers know the value of silence.

Anyone who becomes a successful coinshooter develops a strong state of mind, enabling them to attain goals they would otherwise find impossible. Lucile Bowen and her often-companion in treasure jaunts long ago made up their minds that they could seek treasures as well as any man. They have well proven their point, these Spokane coinshooters who've made themselves known far beyond the Northwest for their charming, persistent searches. A strong mind-set cuts right through age, sex, race, religion, and other such things, and in our hobby-field, a coinshooter or a treasure hunter of one kind or another emerges.

If you want to become proficient at what you seek make up your mind as to what you really want to do. Do you have to stay close to home, because of physical, family, financial, or some other perfectly valid reason? Know your limitations, and then find out how to work within them. After all, a person does not have to leave any given area in order to find much that has been lost or hidden. Treasure is truly everywhere, and in all sorts of unexpected shapes forms, and places. Set your goals, work within your limitations, and be persistent. You will gain much of what you seek! A lucky few will gain even more than what they seek.

Above all, do not set your goals too low. If you allow yourself to hope to find a few coins, and a ring or two, you may soon find that your goal has been reached. Pity the poor soul who seeks a puny goal, and quickly reaches it! That is exactly the problem with people. Too many people never set any real goals, even puny ones, and work diligently toward achieving them. Set your mind, as a sea captain sets sails, and hold firm towards your goals.

Have you read THE TREASURE HUNTER, by Robin Moore and Howard Jennings? You would enjoy it if treasure flows in your veins. It deals with some of Howard Jenning's adventures in South and Central America. The last chapter of the book is pertinent to this discussion, for Jennings therein declares that treasure hunting is not for everybody. He says it is for those who dare to do what they want to do, not for those who seek security. Jennings chose a rootless freedom instead of "third-class 'cradle-to-grave' security". Not everyone can dare such unprotected searches as has Jennings.

There is no need to take off for foreign parts, but there is a need to set your frame of mind. If you spend all your time with job, family, and other obligations, and hope to seek treasure on a weekend or two out of the year, and that not very far from home, forget it. If you can carefully plan out those few weekends, and those only, but are prepared for them, then do not forget it. Those few days could be the best days of your life. They could well enable you to seek more such days, too.

If your job is more important than treasure, to its virtual exclusion, you will never be a treasure seeker. That goes for anything else. If seeking treasure is important to you, you will find some time for its pursuit. Your state of mind will force you to somehow find the time, the money, and anything else you may need.

You don't need to run away from your wife to seek treasure. Take her with you. Floyd and Bettye Abbott have become one of the most successful man and wife coinshooting teams in the country. Ask about these two along the Illinois/Iowa borderlands, and usually they will be known if you're talking to a coinshooter. These folks <u>know</u> what they want to do with their available time. They enjoy doing it together.

For many coinshooters today time, distance, and expense must be limited. There are families. There are jobs. There are children. Bills must be met. Obligations must be fulfilled. That is why coinshooting has become the major area of the entire hobby field. It can be enjoyed even though far places and great caches most often remain wild, lovely dreams. Coinshooting has become a viable compromise between desire and reality.

There are treasures in Lebanon, but one could well get shot there. So hunt your local parks. Peru, Columbia, and Ecuador fairly reek of Incan wealth, but nobody likes South American jails. Local school yards can be very rewarding. Western Europe abounds in Roman, Medieval, and various nationalistic treasures, but our shrinking dollars don't buy as much over there as they used to do. Old carnival sites, picnic areas, and abandoned camp grounds are closer to home, and keep yielding coins. Thus we compromise our dreams with stark reality. We dream smaller, and closer to home, and usually come up with smaller recoveries.

Small recoveries mount up, though, often to surprisingly large sums. Those smaller adventures at least make the treadmills we run at least somewhat more bearable.

What have you done, to improve your state of mind? Have you looked carefully at your "restrictions", to see if perhaps opportunities have been overlooked? Have you thought smaller in area and deeper, since you cannot go afar, not even often out of town?

The following suggestions are not the end-all miracles, but they may be helpful. They are not even really new, not to long-time coinshooters, but they may assist you in helping your own mind help you.

Such a list, of course, must become only a part of your own, for every person and every community is different. Such ideas as these, used, become a part of one's individual frame of mind, and enables that person to become a better seeker of treasure.

* Has dirt from a good location been moved somewhere else? Find out where, and hunt it, if you can. Resodding, excavation, and snow removal often present some possibly rewarding hunting.

* Look across the street from good hunting sites. Bus stops and places where kids have long waited to be picked up. These are sometimes silver mines.

* Search beneath shrubs. They often were not always there, and too many searchers tend to overlook hard-to-search places.

* Look where things were. Old clotheslines, parking meters, old trees. Pathways sodded over. Entryways, exits.

* Return to prime spots. Keep the trash picked up. A good coinshooter can develp a "route", and recover a great many clad coins.

* Use low vegetation periods. Believe it or not, lawnmowers, scythes, and other cutting tools can be important treasure hunting equipment. You can thereby make you own low vegetaion conditions in prime areas.

* Search grounds where homes are being removed or destroyed.
* Use moist conditions to their best advantage. Detection is best during moist periods.

* Old lovers' lanes are great! Those kids had their minds on other things than money.

* The parkings between sidewalk and street. There's money there.

* Have you talked to older people about where folks used to congregate? Do so! It's often the best re-

search time you will ever spend. Don't just think about this, do it.

* Make your own list, and continually enlarge it.

* Study some coin books. Know values of the really good coins you may find. There's no use getting silver prices for coins with additional numismatic value. An old quarter may be worth $1.00 as silver, $20.00 as a collector item.

* Set some definite goals for yourself. Go to some definite site during a definite time. Know ahead of time the sorts of things you're looking for. Was the ghost town booming during certain years, was a certain thing produced there, were there so many people there at such and such a time? Know what you are looking for, even if it is not a certain large cache.

* Last in this list, know your detector(s). Know what the instrument is telling you, know its limitations. The right detector in the wrong place is useless.

The list could, and should, go on. It is up to you, however, to set your own state of mind. Like a computer, your mind is only as good as what is put into it, and how well it is used. If you sit before the hypnotic tube, and dream during commercials of great finds in far places, your successes as a coinshooter will be most limited. Practice with your detectors, do unending research, and set definite goals, and you will amaze yourself.

Coinshooting is one of today's greatest adventures. It can free many people from an otherwise humdrum existence, awakening long-dormant minds and stirring unexercised bodies. Even though great finds are never made, the true coinshooter will be well-rewarded. That person will have tried. Horizons will expand. Though not a day will be added to that person's years, that life will be much longer.

We all have a state of mind. Some expand, ever growing. Some stagnate, shrinking away. How's your state of mind?

THE BIG COVER-UP

If a person is ever to become a coinshooter, to really reach respectable capabilities with a metal detector, that person must become aware of some well-kept secrets. There is a big cover-up out there, facing you, and what you seek is pretty well hidden. The government, local, state, or federal, is not involved here. Big business is not to blame. No terrorist organization is behind it all. Even so, all too many would-be detector users remain mystified by these hidden facts.

The Good Earth is responsible for this cover-up, actually, aided by Time and Weather. The job is so well done, and has been done well for such a long time, that the magic electronic wand had to come along to help unravel the mystery. If coins were not covered up so effectively, there would be no need for detectors. Most coins would be picked up soon after they were lost, and few indeed would remain lost for long.

Being heavy, however, in comparison to the soils and vegetaion upon which they fall, coins usually soon disappear from casual sight. The cover-up begins. Vegetation, dust, sand, leaves, or whatever, moves above them. Mashed into loose or muddy soils, coins simply vanish from sight. Nothing magical, it just seems that way.

A good detector, used correctly, can "see" through such cover-ups. At the risk of repetition of what has been said often by many, too many folks just never learn to use a detector correctly. Or, if they do learn, they just do not take advantage of what they have learned.

Hasty, careless searching is undoubtedly the worst culprit.   Not going to the right sorts of places must follow close behind. Weak batteries and weak thinking both can be easily remedied, but seldom are.

Area, in itself, makes finding buried coins somewhat difficult. There are over three million square miles in the United States. A square mile has 640 acres. Have you ever really tried to carefully and completely check one acre with a metal detector? Many parks of that area have produced coins for several coinshooters for a considerable time, and continue to do so. Therefore, it behooves one to first of all choose carefully before beginning to detect.

Not only must one go to where the most coins are apt to be lost, one must go where the fewest other coin seekers have been searching. That's where the cover-up can help you instead of hurting. There's more than mere dirt over those coins.

Don't despair. That does not mean you must go to the farthest Alaskan tundra, nor fight your way back into the slimiest reaches of mosquito-infested swamps, nor trek out into the most desolate desert you can find. That, after all, would be ignoring the cardinal rule of going where most people go. Most other people don't usually go to those and similar places afar. Where you want to seek is probably not far from where you have already been looking.

There's more to coin cover-up than some grassroots, a pinch of clay, a handful of sand, and a few old leaves. Depth, time, change in usage, erosion, depostion, and ground cover are all contributors to that coin cover-up, yet often these things are virtually ignored. The same old park is hurriedly gone

over, with usually not even too many new coins as a
result. It can scarcely be believed when someone else
comes up with a Mercury dime or a Vnickel there, let
alone the seated dime still another day. Was not
that same park gone over with few or diminished results, time after time?

Back to the basics. Depth. Simply put, the deeper the coin is, the less chance there is to find it,
especially when a detector loop is moved carelessly,
without sufficient overlap, across a surface. This
author has compared a search area to a deep-toothed
saw blade, the detector penetration being at the tip
of those sharp points. Figure it out for yourself.
Items near the top will perhaps be found. A great
deal of area between those sharp little valleys will be
ignored. Coins in those ignored areas will not be
found. Even knowing this, finding all the coins in a
given area is most difficult. Most folks' search patterns just have too broad a sweep with too narrow an
overlap. Often there is no overlap at all. Many
square feet of territory usually remained unscanned
even in areas that fairly good detector users have
tried to carefully scan. The actual scanned area,
even in that carefully scanned surface area, at say
SIX INCHES, is astonishingly small. Remember, we
are talking about inverted cones, almost like lines
across the area you're searching.

Even coming back across that same area at a right
angle does not do it completely. There still will remain square, unsearched areas at a depth. Realizing
this, one can begin to understand how good old coins
can come up from a "worked out" park.

Have you not heard supposedly educated people
begin to mope about being sure that coins do move
up and down? Sure, there's frost heave, and pressure on moist soils, and deposition, and erosion.
Even so, on their own, coins do not rise or sink.
They can be blown, frozen, or washed out. They
can be forced deeper, piled upon, or vibrated deeper
but it does take some external force. Most coins as-
sume a horizontal position, and there they remain unless something moves them.

Several years ago this author spoke of earthworms beetles, rodents, and so forth, and that explanation makes more sense as the years go by. An earthworm eats its way beneath a dime. The dime, being relatively heavy, sinks into that tiny cavity. Gophers, moles, and other such creatures can sink a coin far beyond probable recovery. They also can bring a coin up to the surface, or near it.

Change in usage often fools current coinshooters. What once was a spot for students congregating outside their lecture hall had a few evergreens planted around the edge of it. Years passed, the shrubs spread wider. The new students had less room to congregate, and eventually, even newer students went elsewhere to congregate. Unless the shrubs are some times cut back, or removed, or unless a coinshooter tired of hurrying across the open park forces in between branches, under branches, and looks where nobody else has bothered to look, those coins dropped long ago remain unrecovered.

Have you ever ignored flower beds in the middle or at the edge of a park? Have you ever walked around some thick bushes, time after time? Have you ignored the area where the park attendants throw cut limbs and other such debris?

One good Nebraska coinshooter found such a pile of limbs, and by moving a branch or two at a time, found a silver mine of old coins. A remark by an old timer had clued him into the fact that the very corner now used as a trash pile had once been the site of a summer bazaar, held over many years.

That flower bed may have been once the middle of a playing field. Wait until the flowers have died back, and find out.

The popular, most-used area of a park well may be new. The old section could now be partially a gravelled parking area, grown over with weeds, partially washed out by gully action and ignored, or some other such change of usage and attention. Try to find out about these things in your area. The results can often be startling.

Consideration of erosion can often be helpful. A

slope, for instance, often is a tremendous depository
for coins. Not only do they roll towards the bottom
when lost, they tend to move down the slope through
erosion. A casual search near the bottom may give
meager results, too, for the deposition usually begins
where erosion leaves off. Those coins at the bottom
of a slope may be two or three times deeper than you
think, and no careless search is going to reveal them.

Is there a gullied area near a park or schoolyard
in your area? Have you ever considered the possibility of that area having once been flatter, ungullied,
and used by people? Some such places were once
playing fields, heavily used but poorly cared for.
When erosion became too bad, they were abandoned.

Look carefully along the bottoms of such gullies.
Even intermittent washing can carry coins a considerable distance. Check those edges and slopes, too,
expecially if you begin to find old coins.

Change in usage of an old spot can be profound.
An old playing field, long used far in the past, can
have houses built there. If you find such a situation
and get permission to hunt that yard, or several
yards, the reward can be great.

One very old park, in South Carolina, eventually
had a church built upon it. The politics and other
reasons seem dimmed by the past, and perhaps really
don't matter to the perceptive coinshooters who
discovered that intriguing situation. One grassy
strip, however, some thirty feet wide behind the
church, still actually was a city park. Those astute
coinshooters found colonial coins, Early U. S. coins,
trade tokens, and old jewelry. They came up with
enough old coins from that small area to make many
a coinshooter drool at the very though of it, and to
buy detectors and supply gasoline for some long time
to come.

Good luck? Perhaps, but more likely it was just
seeing a good possibility and checking into it.

Don't be put off by the big cover-up. Overcoming
those problems are what makes this metal detecting so
much fun. Meeting the challenge can be extremely
financially rewarding and enjoyable.

WHERE NOT TO LOOK

At times negative information is extremely valuable. Some negative information concerning coinshooting can be extremely valuable. Any successful coinshooter soon learns that there are good places to look, better places to look, the very best places to look, and plenty of putrid places to look. To be the most successful, simply go to the best places, and avoid the worst places like the plague. It is, of course, not nearly as easy as it sounds. That's why all of us need to keep several negative factors in mind, because coinshooting, thereby, becomes a lot more positive.

One thing we all must keep in mind, perhaps the foremost rule of coinshooting, is that there should be a relatively slow search over a rather small area. The moment a person tries to cover lots of ground, results diminish in both quantity and quality. Haste makes you miss almost every older, deeper coin, no matter what type of detector you are using. Older, deeper coins yield the feebler signals, and those are what a person should be seeking. Larger coins, of course, can indicate near-the-surface coins and other valuables; more often, larger sounds indicate JUNK. If you are wanting surface coins, and many, many of them, use the best discrimination you can get. One time over the area, then you want to go deeper. For sure, the, large signals will indicate JUNK, and you can fairly safely bypass them. This method is not 100% accurate, of course, but it does improve recovery of older and better material.

One place not to look is where you have already searched carefully, at least not for awhile. If you do so, use a detector capable of greater depths, once you have gridded the area with other detectors. Why spend more time seeking diminishing returns in a small place; move over a bit. Use "landmarks" such as trees or rocks as reference points, and work at developing your memory for such details.

When not to search is often more the case than where not to search. Some places are very difficult to detect, at certain times, if not utterly impossible. Any place where large crowds gather, such as at ball games, carnivals, picnics, and several dozen similar congregating areas, are no place to detect when those events are in progress. It simply means avoiding the place when such events are on, and hunting them as soon after the event as possible. A different day, a different season, or even a different time of the day often allows one to hunt even the toughest sorts of places.

Early morning is one of the very best times to coinshoot. If you love to remain in bed, forget all this. Don't even read it, for it may disturb your rest. The early morning hours are quieter, cleaner, and lonlier than any other time of the day, unless one considers say about midnight up until pre-dawn. From just before the sun comes up until people and traffic increase, especially on the weekends, you have the place largely to yourself, as a rule. This is in decent weather, understand, unless you have the physical constitution of a polar bear. It isn't much fun to get up, get frostbitten fingers and toes, have to use a hammer and chisel to check out signals and end up with an Olympic nose. During good, warm weather, however, those early hours of the day cannot be beat for coinshooting.

Don't entirely rule out night hunting. Some coinshooters have been highly successful at night hunting. Some good advice is, let the police know what you are doing, and avoid that possible hassle. Also, know the area in which this night hunting is to be done. Weirder sorts than night-time coinshooters sometimes come out at night and although they probably aren't going to be Dracula, the wolf-man, or Frankenstein's monster, they might be just as wicked or worse. One of this author's spookiest encounters ever was meeting up with some way-out jerk probably high on dope of some kind. None of us need much of that!

The best thing to consider, in knowing where not to search, is to know where people have not often been. In this country, at least, if a field has always been a field, and never a place where people congregate, there will not be as much to find as in more likely spots. There are far more seldom frequented acres than there are the often-used spots, and for coinshooting those are the places to by-pass. We are not talking about the chance find, the cache, the hundreds of thousands to one possibility of coming up with a "biggie", this is coinshooting. If you wish to do your best, avoid the seldom-frequented areas. As one gets farther east, this becomes less and less true, for many a field there was the house place of yesteryear, the ball diamond long-ago abandoned, the picnic ground of the mid-1800's, and no telling what all. Only careful research, then, can tell the best spots. Do not waste your precious time, though, going over relatively barren soil.

Even where people have been, don't go first to the place where they have not had a chance to spend money or where they were not active. A little park across from a store is often far more profitable in recoveries than an even larger, nicer park that is removed from anywhere to buy things. Go where the money is, or was, being spent. Go to the place where people were active. People rolling around in the grass lose money; strollers seldom do.

One place not to search, unless you have permission, is on posted property. There simply are too many places you can search for anyone sneaking onto private property. Trespass is not legal, and by all means, avoid it. Seek permission, and if you cannot get it, find some place else.

One place not to go is a long, long ways from

home; at least not as a regular sort of thing. You can bet your bottom dollar that you do not have to go several counties away to find a good spot. It is most likely, in fact, that you have driven right past a place just as good or better than that one far away, maybe a whole lot better.

Don't go coinshooting unless you want to, and don't go where you don't want to go. Once or twice, perhaps, to please a friend, but don't make a habit of it. The days we have are too precious few to waste them at places or times we don't have a feeling for. How you feel has a lot to do with coinshooting. If you are there to please somebody, you will probably not do very well. If you go where you want, and when you want, you will feel good about it even though you don't find too much.

Don't go where there will be interferences. If traffic by a spot is heavy, there will be noise dulling out signals, smart-alec heckling, and in short, far less than optimum conditions. Remember those early morning hours. If there is a crowd, go when the crowd is gone.

Don't go coinshooting only in the good weather. Bad weather often is the true coinshooter's good weather. It keeps others away from the best spots you hope to search. You can dress for rainy and wet weather, if it is not too wet. You can go hunting in the snow, if the ground beneath is not frozen, and you dress warmly. If it is windy, that is what ear phones are for. Much of that noise is cut out. While others are in hoping for sunshine, you are out making hay while the sun doesn't shine.

Don't go where ground conditions are bad, not if you can help it. That does not mean you can't ever hunt there. If soil is baked like a brick, though, is it always in that condition? How is it right after the frost leaves it in the spring? How is it several days after a rain? Is it like chocolate pudding the day after it rains, and like pavement in four days? What about that second or third day?

Don't go when the vegetation is too high. Not, that is, unless you take along a means of taking care of the vegetation. A power mower, an idiot stick, a plain old scythe, and any number of similar tools make good spots available in lush vegetation conditions. There is such a thing as a "brush hog", if the situation warrants, that will reduce a bramble patch in a hurry.

Just don't go where your efforts will be frustrated and your time wasted. There isn't much point in going to a place where the grass averages two and a half feet in height, poison ivy is rampant, the briars run every which way, including death traps eagerly awaiting the arrival of either of your ankles, and all of it inhabited with a hungry population of blood-sucking, meat-eating, free-riding critters. Such places and times can indefinitely postpone an active coinshooting career.

These negative things should not be negative only. By considering them, your coinshooting will improve, for you won't waste as much time. You will have more energy to go to the better and best spots. By marking off the "baddies" on your list, either mental or real, you can concentrate on the "goodies".

Equally true, you should have a list of do's. It should be as long, if not longer than your what not to do's. There is no reason for any true coinshooter not to have more than enough to do should he or she live several lifetimes. Is that not the way you really want it?

If you and I meet out there, and die off of stroke or whatnot within the same five minutes, can you think of any way you'd rather go? I hope it isn't until I'm at least ninety-seven, for I won't be nearly done with all I hope to do, but I would far rather do that than keep some machine busy in a hospital several years.

Whatever you do, don't do the don'ts, and do do the do's. Most of all, YOU do it. There is no feeling like figuring out that a certain spot should offer some excellent coinshooting experiences, going there, and coming up with some really good finds.

What you sitting there for? I know this little hotspot. . .

THE MAGIC OF COINSHOOTING

Coinshooting comes about as close to practicing magic as a hobbyist can get, short of being a budding new Houdini or Blackstone, an emerging new Einstein or Edison, or a reincarnated DaVinci or Archimedes. Indeed, when an otherwise ordinary person these days bothers to really learn the best ways to use a detector, does the research necessary to locating the prime hunting spots, and goes at the hobby with the patience of Job and the persistence of a donkey-driver, that person becomes extraordinary. That person is as close to being a necromancer, an alchemist of yore, as close to a true magician as anyone can get, these days.

Consider, an alchemist was supposed to search for some means of turning base metal into gold. In spare moments these delvers into the unknown searched for elixirs that would prolong life, or at least make life better. By golly, good coinshooters come much closer to those wild-eyed goals than most alchemists or lifetime necromancers ever came. With some inexpensive batteries in their unit, surely base metal, most coinshooters come up with copper, silver, and even some gold. Usually it's even in the form of coins, already smelted, shaped, and minted. Sometimes it has even been made into jewelry. By adding time and talent to those batteries, along with some modern electronic circuitry, to be sure, up comes some precious metals. Along with it comes an improved life,too, for it's a fairly recognized fact that those who trade rocking chairs in on detectors definitely add zest, and usually time to their lives. The stuff those alchemists gulped down probably shortened theirs!

Is that almost magic, or not?

There is a great deal about coinshooting that smacks of magic, at least to those who aren't familiar with the hobby. It is not so magical to coinshooters well versed in the field. There is the overwhelming number of coins and like valuables awaiting recovery. There is that almost magical moment when something of worth is extracted unexpectedly from the ground, or the equally magical sensation of searching successfully for something important and finding it through diligent effort.

As an example, my friend, Hunter Pritchard found a man's mother's wedding ring in Louisiana a number of years ago. The man had been reluctant to allow Hunter to hunt on the property, but had let him search around an old house there while he watched to see how it was done. When that simple gold band came up, not far from the kitchen steps from where she'd accidentally shaken it off years before, Hunter had the run of the place. If not magic, a pretty fair substitute.

The coinshooter who finds several hundred coins in a morning's or afternoon's searching fulfills the dream of most children, that of magically coming up with one coin after another. What child, and a good many adults, has not thought of finding one coin, then two, and then more and more, until hands and pockets are full. Coinshooting is one way of making that sort of long-time dream become reality.

How many listless retirees have you seen transformed by the magic of a detector into a person with a new lease on life. Anything that can renew a failing person's interest and vitality has to be nearly magic. If you know of someone who could use such therapy, do indeed introduce them to the hobby.

It is amusing to coinshooters to hear government officials and economists talk about people hoarding pennies. If people are smart, they are hoarding them or are starting to, but the real culprit is the loss of tens of million of those coins. The cent is of such little value, now, that few people stoop to pick them up if they see them lying there. Nobody knows, but it is safe to say that far more cents still await recovery than the total piled up in banks, pockets, and hoards. That steady loss has been going on for an awfully long time.

The magic in this is that a good coinshooter can reclaim a good many of these potentially more valuable coppers. All the increasing coinshooting activity of the past few years has not led to the recovery of half of the cents being lost and less than that of the earlier one cent pieces. Yes, a few places have been worked very hard. Some areas now yield very few older cents. The problem is, very few coinshooters really go to all the places where coins were lost. For every playground there are a dozen spots where children once played, but now are forgotten. Go there, for Wheatears, Buffaloes, and Mercs: go there for Standing Liberties, and even the Seated Damsels.

Go to the out of the way for the strongest magic. This author found his nicest two cent piece, an 1865, in Mountain City. That's between Central City and Black Hawk in Colorado, and that coin was probably dropped there in 1865. When the boom was over, they moved out the houses, and plaster fell atop it. It seemed magic, too, when this author came up with a 1919 cent. That's nothing too great, but where it was found meant something. Troops trained for World War I outside of Columbus, New Mexico. Some soldier in his haste to please his drill sergeant, dropped that coin, new, for that was the last year they used that training ground. Or how about the 1892 O half dollar, found at sinful old Cardinal, down below Caribou, Colorado? That's where the shady ladies of the area offered their services, and that half dollar was about the going price, at that time. If finding coins in out of the way spots such as that is not at least next door to magic, then there indeed is no magic left in the world.

Try to locate somebody's ring, sometime, if you've not done so, yet. There is a real eureka feeling when you've come up with a newlywed's ring, or some old person's keepsake. Such feelings transcend monetary reward, although that's nice, too, if you get it. Ask Leo Pavel, up in Nebraska, about good feelings in finding a valuable diamond ring for someone, both moneywise and otherwise. Jim Alexander did the same thing, down in Texas, and that was a Texas-sized diamond. It's probably not true that quantity makes the quality of the magic stronger, for we've all seen some good feelings over recovering some rather insignificant items.

Even so, there is something rather awe-inspiring about the really big finds that have been coming up. Big magic, if you will, which has caused all sorts of attention and furor, usually far more than the finders would have liked to have had.

When Bill and Doris Collins bought a forty acre farm in Iowa, they did not dream of treasure. When a series of hard luck had brought them almost to the end of their rope, breaking into their septic system was about the last straw. Can it be anything but a magical Cinderella story when poor folks, about out of good luck, find 75 gold coins while starting to fix a broken septic system? Two California 49'ers, Englishmen, evidently buried the cache, or Applewood did, on his section of land near Grayville. He fell ill, and died before he could tell his partner, Walton where the money was buried. Walton and others look-ed for it over the years. A septic tank was put in right beside it, evidently without discovering the cache. The magic of it was that in fairy tale manner, people who could really use it, found it.

There's magic in finding part of the Atocha treasure, the Platoro recovery on the Texas coast, and the fabulous recovery on the Silver Shoals. These are not the average run-of-the-mill coinshooting finds, though, but the magic is that it could and does happen to just about anyone. Yes, the next coin probably will be a memorial cent, not too great even if the new zinc cents do come out, but next time. . .

What about the man who found the $20 gold piece on an abandoned northwest race track? Probably worth $300,000, that outing. Or the fellow who came up with a pewter dollar, then worth $16,000, and who knows how much now? Coinshooting brought to the surface of an Iowa farm 14 gold coins--a persistent coinshooter listened to a tale of folks returning from the California gold fields getting wiped out by a tornado, and gold coins being found when the bodies were buried. These sorts of finds may not be commonplace, but they are going on all the time. If there is not something magical about never knowing what will next come up, a great many treasure hunters mistakingly have a sense of anticipation not found in many other hobby fields.

It is rather mystifying how coins can stay in the ground as long as they do, and suffer so little damage. Copper coins suffer the most, as a rule, with nickels nearly as bad. Badly acidic soils do the most damage, although the abrasion of sand can eventually erase all detail from a coin. Gold, except in terribly corrosive situations, is very little affected at all. Pulling out a seemingly new gold coin, that nevertheless was lost sixty, a hundred, or more years ago, has to be an exciting peak in any coinshooter's life. Silver, too, does well over the years. Silver does pit from soil acids, darken if exposed to the sun, or begin to eat away if in conditions such as sulphur-laden ground. In well-drained soils, though, even a very, very old silver coin comes out remarkably well.

Don't you wish the government was still making these gems? The government won't, of course, as long as people put up with the debased tokens now passed off as money. Coinshooters may magically retrieve these beautiful coins of yesteryear, but it will take more than magic to force the government to begin to mint silver coins again. Not when they now intend to even do away with copper.

The coinshooter, of course, has a stupendous advantage over the rest of the population. He or she can go out and with those mystifying electronics, keep coming up with copper, silver, and even gold coins. The 14K ring you find today may well be worth a dozen or more times what you could sell it for right now, given a minimal inflation rate. You can sell that ring now, probably, for more than someone once bought it for in a jewelry store. Don't foolishly cast aside these magic keepsakes for constantly shrinking in value Federal Reserve notes: Don't sell your coins unless you have to. Magically, your play today could well be your pay tomorrow.

If copper cents become worth 3¢, or 5¢, or perchance 10¢, would you not like to have saved 50,000 of them? Silver dimes can now be sold for a dollar, more or less. If, though, silver goes to $100 per ounce, and there are many indications that it could do so, and double that over the longer term, that silver dime would sell for ten dollars or more. As for gold, no few people believe that gold must eventually go for at least $1000 per ounce in the reasonably near future, and if metalic backing of money returns to prevent absolute monetary collapse, $3000 per ounce on up. In that scenario, even the short-term picture, many coinshooters would indeed be glad they had mastered a bit of magic.

So, you coinshooters/alchemists out there, practice your craft. Indulge in those spells of fascination Change the base metal of your batteries into valuable coins and jewelry. Pursue your magic electronic wand, and observe how a find here and there becomes an ever-growing cache, with you a veritable sorcerer's apprentice unleashing a steady stream of coins. Ho, the copper ring of power, sweeping the ground to detect the pieces of yesteryear. Presto, the electronic circuitry making us aware of unseen treasures. Magic? Yes, there is a magic in coinshooting!